"How would you answer the question, What's the main message of the Bible? How does the Bible itself answer that question? Introducing readers to biblical theology, Bruno teases out answers to these questions from Scripture, methodically tracing the major milestones of redemptive history to illuminate the gospel thread and to tie it all together. Whether you're new to the Bible or have grown up hearing its stories in Sunday school, Bruno's book will lead you to a greater love for God's Word and hope in the Savior to whom every part of it points."

J. Mack Stiles, CEO, Gulf Digital Solutions; General Secretary, Fellowship of Christian UAE Students (FOCUS), United Arab Emirates; author, *Evangelism*

"This compact and insightful book is ideal for one-on-one discipleship, as well as more formal teaching contexts. All Christians, whether mature or young in the faith, will find much to meditate on and rejoice in as Bruno faithfully sketches in the story of redemption."

Thomas R. Schreiner, James Buchanan Harrison Professor of New Testament Interpretation, The Southern Baptist Theological Seminary

"In order to understand our Bibles, we need to understand the big story of God's redemptive plan. Chris Bruno focuses on sixteen key texts to provide a clear and accessible outline of this big story. I recommend the book highly."

Douglas J. Moo, Wessner Chair of Biblical Studies, Wheaton College

"Chris Bruno captures the plotline of the Bible in sixteen short verses. Each verse is vital for understanding the unfolding story, but the story is also greater than the sum of its parts. When seen together, the cumulative picture is breathtaking and life changing."

Jason C. Meyer, Pastor for Preaching and Vision, Bethlehem Baptist Church, Minneapolis, Minnesota

"Chris Bruno's book leads us through the Bible as a whole story in just sixteen verses. It gives us a secure grasp of the overall unity of the message of the Bible through accessible chapters and bite-size portions of the text."

Josh Moody, Senior Pastor, College Church, Wheaton, Illinois; author, *Journey to Joy: The Psalms of Ascent*

The Whole Story of the Bible in 16 Verses

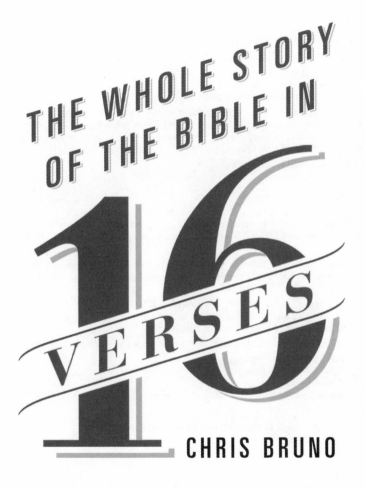

THE WHOLE STORY
OF THE BIBLE IN
16
VERSES

CHRIS BRUNO

CROSSWAY

WHEATON, ILLINOIS

The Whole Story of the Bible in 16 Verses

Copyright © 2015 by Christopher R. Bruno

Published by Crossway
        1300 Crescent Street
        Wheaton, Illinois 60187

Cover design: Dual Identity, inc.

First printing 2015

Printed in the United States of America

Unless otherwise indicated, all Scripture quotations are from the ESV® Bible (*The Holy Bible, English Standard Version®*), copyright © 2001 by Crossway, a publishing ministry of Good News Publishers. Used by permission. All rights reserved.

Scripture quotations marked NASB are from *The New American Standard Bible®*. Copyright © The Lockman Foundation 1960, 1962, 1963, 1968, 1971, 1972, 1973, 1975, 1977, 1995. Used by permission.

Scripture references marked NIV are taken from The Holy Bible, New International Version®, NIV®. Copyright © 1973, 1978, 1984, 2011 by Biblica, Inc.™ Used by permission. All rights reserved worldwide.

All emphases in Scripture quotations have been added by the author.

Trade paperback ISBN: 978-1-4335-4282-4
ePub ISBN: 978-1-4335-4285-5
PDF ISBN: 978-1-4335-4283-1
Mobipocket ISBN: 978-1-4335-4284-8

Library of Congress Cataloging-in-Publication Data
Bruno, Chris, 1980-
   The whole story of the Bible in 16 verses / Chris
Bruno.
      pages cm
   Includes bibliographical references and index.
   ISBN 978-1-4335-4282-4 (tp)
   1. Bible—Introductions. 2. Bible—Quotations.
I. Title.
BS475.3.B79   2015
220.6'1—dc23   2014027306

Crossway is a publishing ministry of Good News Publishers.

VP		25	24	23	22	21	20	19	18	17	16	15
15	14	13	12	11	10	9	8	7	6	5	4	3	2	1

To Luke, Simon, and Elliot

May you enter this story with
joy in the Promised One, Jesus

Contents

Preface

If you are reading this book, you are interested in biblical theology, even if you don't know it yet. Unlike systematic theology, which gathers together everything the Bible teaches about a particular subject into one place, biblical theology is concerned with unpacking the chronological development of a theme or cluster of themes in the Bible. The goal is to trace a particular theme or the overall storyline as it unfolds in the Bible. In this book, we are going to trace the storyline of the Bible and look at how some of the central themes are developed throughout its pages. So congratulations—you are on your way to becoming a biblical theologian!

Some biblical theology books are forest books. They paint with broad strokes, showing us the main parts from one section of the Bible or even the big picture of the whole Bible. These kinds of books help us see the overall shape of the Bible's main themes. Other biblical theology books are tree books. They take one tree—either a theme or a passage from the Bible—and carefully saw it apart, count the rings, and then give us a thorough explanation of how that particular tree fits into the forest. But there aren't a lot of books—especially shorter books, like this one—that are both forest and tree books.

This book is an attempt to see the forest by looking at the trees (verses or passages). While we won't look at the trees as closely as some books, we will look at sixteen important trees (we might even call them guideposts) that will help us get a sense of the whole forest. After this short tour through the forest of the Bible, I hope you will be excited about finding a few forest books and a few tree books to help you get a better grasp of the story of the Bible both in its whole and in its parts.

So let's set out on our journey together. We will start at the very beginning, with the creation of the world.

Acknowledgments

This book began in a Thursday night class at the Antioch School Hawai'i, the pastoral training program I helped lead. In those two hours, we worked through most of the texts that ended up in this book. John Boehm, John Curran, Dustin and Britt Harris, Nathan Kawanishi, Todd Morikawa, Alton Uyema, Mark Watanabe, and Justin White—thank you for helping me trace this story. Thanks also to the congregation of Christ Fellowship Church in Sun Prairie, Wisconsin, where I presented some of this material. My church, Harbor Church, and fellow elders, John Boehm, Matt Dirks, Justin Geer, and Ethan Pien, have been a constant joy and support to my family and me. Many other friends in ministry at the Antioch School Hawai'i, at the Northland International University, and scattered around the world have encouraged and sharpened me as I worked on this book. Special thanks are also due to Jim and Chelsea Pferschy, David Griffiths, and my wife, Katie Bruno, for valuable feedback as I prepared this manuscript. Finally, thanks to the folks at Crossway, and in particular Dave DeWit and Greg Bailey, for their editorial help and commitment to God-glorifying, gospel-driven Christian books. I pray this book approaches that high standard.

While I did not cite them in specific places, men such as Graeme Goldsworthy, Tom Schreiner, Greg Beale, and a host of others shaped the way I understand biblical theology. Though it may not have been as evident, men such as John Piper and

Doug Moo, along with John Calvin, have shaped the way that I read the Bible and do biblical exegesis. I am deeply thankful for their influence in person and on the page.

My wife, Katie, and sons are nothing but supportive of all the things God has called me to do. They also constantly remind me of what is most important. It is my prayer that my boys will know and love this story, and that their lives will be shaped by it. Because of that hope, I am dedicating this book to my sons, Luke, Simon, and Elliot.

PART 1

THE TIME IS COMING

CREATION

And behold, it was very good.

Genesis 1:31

Our view of the world begins with our view of God. The way we think about God shapes the way we think about everything else, along with the way we act and respond to every circumstance. Because of this, we need to get our thoughts about God straight at the beginning of our journey. In other words, as we set out to tell the story of the Bible, we have to begin with God. He is the Author of the Bible and the hero of every story found in it, so we can't even think about telling the story without starting with him.

To do this, we are going to start at the last verse of the first chapter of the Bible, which says:

> And God saw everything that he had made, and behold, it was very good. And there was evening and there was morning, the sixth day. (Gen. 1:31)

At first glance, Genesis 1 doesn't seem to give us much information about God. Instead, it seems as if we have just the story of creation, with the existence of God more or less assumed. But as we read through the account of the creation week in the first chapter of the Bible, the authority of God is pretty astonishing. God speaks, and things happen. If you have ever been in the room with a CEO, a senator, or maybe even the president, you've seen what happens when a person of authority speaks. Things happen, and they happen quickly. With God, we can see this same principle at work—multiplied by about a million.

If you aren't familiar with the creation story, let me summarize it: God made everything, and everything he made was good. We don't need to go much further to get the point. In the beginning, there was nothing, and God made everything just by speaking. He spoke, and creation obeyed. It obeyed by coming into being, by sprouting every living thing, and finally by submitting itself to God's sovereign power. The emphasis in the whole chapter, and especially in verse 31, is the ease with which God spoke the world into being and the harmony that existed between Creator and creation.

So at the very beginning, we meet a God who is able to create everything that exists with seemingly no more effort than it takes you or me to tie our shoes. We meet a God whose creative power and authority extend to every part of the universe.

When he had finished making everything, God looked at it all and saw that it was "very good." Notice that God was the One who pronounced the verdict. The entire universe came to be because he spoke, and he was the only one qualified to evaluate his creative work. We don't see the angels coming alongside God to give him some encouraging feedback. (In fact, we don't even know when and how God created the angels, though we can be pretty sure they started praising him right away.) No, the focus at the very beginning is on God, his creation, and his authority over that creation.

When we put together God's power to create and his authority to evaluate his creation, we find that God is the sovereign Ruler of the universe. In other words, God is the King who has the right, the power, and the authority to rule over his creation. And the King's official decree over his kingdom is that it is "very good."

Isn't this kind of surprising, when we stop and think about it? If we look around our world or turn on the news, the world doesn't seem "very good." Everything is decaying, everyone is fighting, and no one seems to know how to fix anything. How, then, could God say this?

You don't have to be a Hebrew scholar to understand the meaning of this phrase in its context. First, we can see that God's declaration applied to *everything* that he had made. It's not as if just one part of the creation was good, another part was just okay, and still another part was kind of crummy. No, in the beginning, every part of the creation was good.

Second, not only was the creation good, it was *very* good. We are not talking about average work. I don't know about you, but whenever I try to create something with my hands, I can never quite get it right. I remember putting together a model Corvette when I was in middle school. The picture on the box displayed a sleek and shiny sports car—it looked even better than the real thing. But when I put the model together, the glue clumped up and the paint job looked like a four-year-old had done it. It was certainly not everything it was intended to be!

Even the best of our creative efforts lack something. Many musicians (of which I am not) consider Ludwig van Beethoven's *Fifth Symphony* one of the best and most important musical scores in history. But after its premiere, not many people gave it much attention. The orchestra had time to rehearse it only once before the performance, and at one point the musicians flubbed it so badly that Beethoven literally stopped the music and made them start over. Not many people pronounced the symphony "very good" after that first performance. But when God pronounced the creation "very good," he meant that it was everything he intended it to be.

This doesn't just mean that it was beautiful or awe-inspiring, though we can be sure that it was (and often still is). When God said the creation was "very good," he was proclaiming that his creation was doing what he wanted it to do. Trees were growing where they should, fish were swimming the right way, and humans were relating to each other, the creation, and their Creator just as he intended (we'll come back to that in the next chapter). In short, God's kingdom was in perfect harmony with its King.

While you probably know that a couple of stops down the line we will see this perfect harmony broken, it is plain to see that God's creation still reflects his mighty power. Think about the most beautiful place you have ever visited. For me, this is probably the Na Pali coast on the Hawaiian island of Kauai. Imagine a sixteen-mile stretch of towering green cliffs, dotted with waterfalls, some as high as four thousand feet above the ocean. When you sit on a small boat in the water looking up at these mountains, you feel very small. But you also see that God's creation can still be very good. Maybe for you it is the vastness of a canyon, the view from the top of a mountain, the wonder of an untouched field the morning after a snowstorm, or any one of a thousand other aspects of nature. We don't always see this when we look out our windows to see trash in the gutter or snow that is black with dirt, but God made the world to be "very good."

In Psalm 104, we can see that the earth, the sky, and the ocean, along with all they contain, continue to reflect his creative power and mighty authority. And verse 27 concludes, "These all look to you." In spite of all that has gone wrong, God's kingdom still looks to him and depends on him, just as it has from the very beginning.

Before we leave this first tree in our tour through the forest, it's important that we insist on the ongoing goodness of God's creation. Paul reminds us in 1 Timothy 4:4 that "everything created by God is good." He doesn't say that *most* things created by God are good. He also doesn't say that everything created by God *was* good. No, Paul affirms that God's entire creation is still good.

I can understand why some people disparage the "physical world" and hope to escape to the purely "spiritual world." After all, it's not hard to find problems in the world today! But if we claim to have a truly biblical view of God's creation, then we must continue to insist that God's created work is good and that he has a purpose for it.

On the flip side, we also can't forget that the world is not an end in and of itself. We cannot speak of the creation apart from the God who made it—and who not only made it, but also has authority over it and upholds it by his sovereign power. So if we are seeking the good of the created order (as we perceive it) to be the highest virtue in the universe, then we haven't seen the whole picture. Instead, we have to affirm that its goodness depends on God, the Maker and King of creation.

Genesis 1:31 gives us a window into the creation story, but it is not the whole story. Even though God is the King of his creation, he doesn't want to rule it alone. But to tell that part of the story, we need to move to our next tree.

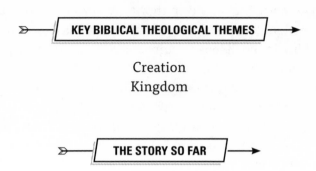

KEY BIBLICAL THEOLOGICAL THEMES

Creation
Kingdom

THE STORY SO FAR

God created a kingdom, and he is the King.

HUMAN BEINGS

In the image of God . . . he created them.

Genesis 1:27–28

The famous sixteenth-century theologian John Calvin wrote that almost all of our wisdom consists of knowledge of God and knowledge of self. In the first chapter, we learned something about God in his creation and rule of the world. As we move to the second stop on our tour through the Bible, we will get a glimpse of some truths we must know about ourselves. So before we leave the creation week behind, we need to back up to look at the important description of God's creation and commission of the human race:

> So God created man in his own image,
>> in the image of God he created him;
>> male and female he created them.

And God blessed them. And God said to them, "Be fruitful and multiply and fill the earth and subdue it, and have dominion over the fish of the sea and over the birds of the heavens and over every living thing that moves on the earth." (Gen. 1:27–28)

In spite of his sovereign power and absolute right to rule his creation, God chose not to do it alone. Instead, he created Adam and Eve as the pinnacle of creation. While lots of Christians disagree about the best interpretation of Genesis 1–2, it's hard to avoid the conclusion that God created Adam and Eve for a specific role: to serve as his image bearers, or representatives, in the creation.

When we consider what it means to be made in the image of God, it doesn't take long to get lost in the maze of theological discussion. Scholars have debated the meaning of these verses for centuries, so we can't (and don't need to) unpack all of those arguments here. But we do need to consider a couple of key options.

Some argue that the image of God has to do primarily with our ability to use reason and intellect. Others argue that the image of God is tied to our ability to relate to God and others. Still others say that it is linked to the task and commission that God gave to Adam and Eve. But it is most likely that the image of God is bound up in both the characteristics *and* the relational tendencies that we share with God.

In the ancient world, an image of one of the pagan gods would be placed in a temple in order to represent that god. While there is not a one-for-one parallel between that practice and the idea of the image of God, we can say that we too are God's representatives on earth. This doesn't mean that we walk around worshiping each other or leaving oranges for each other, like we might see in front of one of those little Buddha statues at a Chinese restaurant. Instead, it means that we are *able* to fulfill the commission he has given to us. So being made in the image of God meant that Adam and Eve were able to do what God had called them to do.

Also, notice that *both* Adam and Eve were created in the image of God. Its important to see that the word translated "man" in verse 27 applies to both men and women. And just in case we might misunderstand, God clarifies that both men and women are included in the group that he made in his image. When we remember the common mistreatment of women in the ancient world, this becomes even more important. It means that, while men and women have specific roles God has designed them for, we cannot say that only men (or only women) get to be called the image of God. Both were called to play a role in God's good creation.

In our text, this role has two important parts. First, God called Adam and Eve to fill the earth and subdue it. While this command obviously included the expectation that Adam and Eve were to have children, there was a little more to it. If we look carefully at the parallel account of the creation in Genesis 2, we see a little hint at what it meant for Adam and Eve to subdue the earth. Genesis 2:8 tells us that God planted a garden in Eden, in the east. And God chose to make that garden the particular place where he met with his people. The implication is that there was lots of room outside of the garden in Eden and in the rest of the world where neither he nor his people lived.

Can you see what this commission implies? When Adam and Eve were called to subdue the earth, they were called to expand the garden. But this was not just some ancient form of suburban sprawl. Instead, it was a command to expand the territory where God himself lived. In other words, as they had children and their children had children, they were charged with expanding the dominion where God dwelt with his people.

It is almost as if the garden was a little temple in Eden, and God's images were commanded to expand that garden-temple to fill Eden, then the east, and eventually the whole world. As the garden expanded, the dwelling place of God with his people would slowly expand with it.

But the primary emphasis of the commission, even here at the very beginning, was not on the place that they would be expanding, but rather on the purpose for the place. God made the man and woman to be his image bearers, and as his image bearers, their job was to make his glory and his blessing known. So what we are actually seeing is that God commissioned Adam and Eve to be the first missionaries.

The other part of their commission was that Adam and Eve were to "have dominion" over the earth and, in particular, the animals. Some Christians and many non-Christians have misinterpreted this second part of the commission. They make accusations that this is a license for people to destroy the environment, to scorch the earth and then move on to the next patch of land. But if we take time to really think about what is going on in these verses, it is obvious that this is a perverted way of reading them.

It is crucial for us to connect this part of the commission to the image of God. Being made in God's image meant that Adam and Eve were supposed to be his representatives on the earth. And since he is the sovereign King over all creation, his representatives rule on his behalf. So to exercise dominion over the earth does not mean that we use it and abuse it. Is this the way we would expect God, who called his creation "very good," to rule the earth?

The command to have dominion meant that Adam and Eve were to rule the animals and the rest of the earth in the way that God himself would rule them. They were to care for them, to be good stewards of them, and to bring glory to God in the way they ruled over them.

In our postcolonial, anti-imperial world, we have a jaded view of what it is like to be under the authority of a good and wise king. Given the abuses we've seen from monarchs and dictators even in the last century, we can understand this mistrust. But at the beginning, it wasn't this way. God was a good King, and he created Adam and Eve to echo his loving rule in his creation-kingdom.

In fact, the creation of Adam and Eve, God's image bearers, gives us a good picture of the rest of the creation week. He made the first humans to represent him in this very good creation, to expand the dwelling place where his glory would be on display, and to rule that dwelling place on his behalf.

This also means that God was entering into a special kind of agreement with his people when he created them. He made Adam and Eve, gave them life, and placed them in the garden. He then called them to these important tasks. Many theologians call this special relationship *a covenant*. We will unpack that idea more as it is revealed in the history of salvation, but it is important to introduce this concept at the very beginning. From the very first day of creation, God has been committed to his creation and has had a covenantal love for mankind in particular.

But as we look around and see that something is wrong with the way human beings interact with creation, we have to conclude that somewhere along the way, someone dropped the ball. That leads us to our next stopping point: the fall.

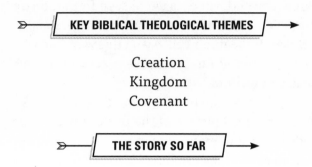

KEY BIBLICAL THEOLOGICAL THEMES

Creation
Kingdom
Covenant

THE STORY SO FAR

God created a kingdom, and he is the King, but he made human beings to represent him in that kingdom.

THE FALL

She took of its fruit and ate.

Genesis 3:6–7

At this point, you might be asking, if God made everything to be good, and he created human beings to rule over his good creation, then why is the world so broken? This question leads us to Genesis 3. This chapter is one of the most heartbreaking in the entire Bible, because in it, we see God's good creation turn rotten. In it, we see Adam and Eve, whom God made to love and trust him, and to rule on his behalf, turn their backs on him. And the saddest part of all is that every one of us can see ourselves reflected in Adam and Eve.

To tell this part of the story, we need to back up into chapter 2 and introduce a little detail that I left out earlier. When God created and commissioned Adam and Eve, he gave them virtually free rein in the garden. Under him, they were its rulers, and they had the right and privilege to eat from nearly every tree in the garden. But there was one tree—just one—from which God said they could not eat. God told them, "Of the tree of the knowledge of good and evil you shall not eat, for in the day that you eat of it you shall surely die" (Gen. 2:17).

We don't know many details about this tree. We don't know exactly what made this tree so special or why God prohibited them from eating its fruit as opposed to that of the hundreds of others in the garden. And, with all due respect to John Milton, author of the classic *Paradise Lost*, we don't know if it was an apple that Eve ate.

What we do know about this tree and God's command not to eat from it is that God was protecting Adam and Eve. When we go back to the idea of a covenant relationship, an important part of such a relationship is defining the conditions that come with it.

Of course, it is important to define the terms in any relationship. Failure to do so has been the source of much teenage angst in modern America. Even when we are a little older and married, an important rule of thumb is that we have to articulate our expectations, right? (Please don't ask my wife if I have mastered that one yet.)

So as part of the covenant relationship between God and human beings, God asked them to trust him and obey him. He asked them to believe that what he told them was the best thing for them—just like you or I tell our kids to wear a helmet, watch for cars, or slow down when they are riding their bikes. But how do our kids often respond? They doubt our advice and act as if they know better than those in authority over them—just as Adam and Eve did here. In fact, our kids act as they do because Adam and Eve acted as they did! We'll come back to that later.

At the beginning of Genesis 3, we discover that a creature called "the Serpent" made his way into the garden. Just like the tree, we don't know much about him. We don't know if Eve was surprised to hear the Serpent talk; after all, she made it her habit to walk with God in the cool part of the day, so I'm not sure we are good judges of what would or wouldn't have surprised her (see Gen. 3:8). But we know the Serpent started a conversation with Eve, and that Adam did not protect his wife from the Serpent. So he probably wasn't doing the greatest job of subduing the earth.

If Adam wasn't doing a great job subduing the earth, it's also pretty clear that Eve wasn't doing the greatest job fulfilling the commission either, because as soon as the Serpent asked her a question, she told a lie. Instead of just repeating God's command not to eat from the tree, Eve added that God had told them not to touch it! When the Serpent saw that opening, he was quick to pounce on it, and he convinced Eve that instead of putting the covenant stipulations in place to protect her and her husband, God had commanded them not to eat from the tree to prevent them from being truly happy.

Again, this story sounds really familiar. How often do you hear from others or, more likely, from yourself that God's commands are designed to kill your joy? This ancient story is actually very relevant:

> So when the woman saw that the tree was good for food, and that it was a delight to the eyes, and that the tree was to be desired to make one wise, she took of its fruit and ate, and she also gave some to her husband who was with her, and he ate. Then the eyes of both were opened, and they knew that they were naked. And they sewed fig leaves together and made themselves loincloths. (Gen. 3:6–7)

While we tend to think of these two verses as humanity's first sin, if you tracked closely with the first part of the chapter, you probably saw that Adam and Eve were already gone. Their story is like one of those rare times when Barry Sanders, the great running back for the Detroit Lions, actually got the blocks to have a clear running lane. You knew he was going to reach the end zone even when he was still at the 30-yard line. In the same way, by the time Eve actually looked at the tree and noticed how delightful it really was, there was no turning back.

The Serpent convinced Eve to take the fruit by convincing her that when she and Adam ate it, they would be like God, knowing good and evil. So she turned and looked at the tree, perhaps seeing it in a new light. It was "good for food" and "a delight to the eyes." This means that the fruit of the tree wasn't some dried-up little fig or green banana. We don't know how long it had been since God had created Adam and Eve, but since they didn't have children, it had probably been less than a year. Maybe Eve was seeing this fruit tree ripen for the first time. Seeing the beauty of the tree and its fruit, she may have been tempted to value it, the creation, more highly than she valued God, its Creator.

But she also saw that the tree was "desired to make one wise." Remember what the Serpent had told her? Her desire to be wise like God welled up, and she could no longer resist. So she took the fruit and ate it.

Then she turned and gave it to her husband, Adam. Sometimes we picture Adam off somewhere collecting nuts or something while Eve was tempted, then coming home to find a forbidden fruit casserole in the oven. But look closely: "she also gave some to her husband who was with her." Adam was standing with her the whole time! Not only had he failed to subdue the earth, but he stood idly by while the Serpent convinced his wife to defy God's command. In fact, he was a willing and able participant in this treason. He was just as quick to take the fruit and eat it. So don't be too quick to pin this one on Eve alone. They were both guilty, and both had to face the consequences of their actions. And those consequences would be severe. In *Paradise Lost*, Milton described sin and death as the "hellish pair." They were inseparable. Once sin arrived, death appeared, "close following pace for pace."[1]

God had told them that "in the day that you eat of it you shall surely die" (Gen. 2:17), and this is exactly what happened. While the death of their physical bodies would come one day as a result of their sin, the death they faced on that day was more serious. It was a spiritual death, a death to their intimacy with their God and Creator. They were no longer able to walk with God in the cool of the day. The fellowship and relationship they had shared with him was severed. Eventually he threw them out of the garden and never again allowed them to enter (Gen. 3:23–24).

After they ate the fruit, they knew they were naked and experienced the shame and even fear that comes from such nakedness. So they made loincloths for themselves. They wanted to cover themselves, to hide from each other, and to hide from God. But their pitiful garments could not hide their sin from God. He found them and pronounced judgment upon them.

But even in the midst of this darkness, we find notes of hope. God did not leave Adam and Eve naked (Gen. 3:21). He provided them with clothes, and in so doing, he gave them a picture of the redemption he would provide for them.

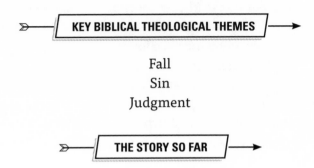

KEY BIBLICAL THEOLOGICAL THEMES

Fall

Sin

Judgment

THE STORY SO FAR

God created a kingdom, and he is the King, but he made human beings to represent him in that kingdom. Adam and Eve rejected this call.

REDEMPTION PROMISED

He shall bruise your head.

Genesis 3:15

If you have been a Christian for very long, you may know the lyrics to William Cowper's hymn "God Moves in a Mysterious Way."[2] Possibly the most meaningful and moving lyrics from that hymn are these: "Behind a frowning providence he hides a smiling face." Even if the hymn is new to you, the sentiment behind it most likely is not, because Cowper is simply restating the truth found in well-known verses such as Romans 8:28: "And we know that for those who love God all things work together for good, for those who are called according to his purpose." While this cannot mean that God will make "every day a Friday" or give you "your best life now," it does mean that we must never lose hope in God's commitment to make all things that have gone wrong right again.

The blueprint for that hope is introduced in Genesis 3:15, just after what seems to be the worst possible turn of events. God says:

And I will put enmity
Between you and the woman,
And between your seed and her seed;
He shall bruise you on the head,
And you shall bruise him on the heel. (NASB)

In the midst of what looks like a very dark providence, God's smiling face shines through in the most amazing way. We saw at the end of our last chapter the hopeful note of God clothing Adam and Eve. But beyond that, even as God cursed humanity and the Serpent for his role in Adam and Eve's treasonous act, God gave hope to them and their family line. It was as if God was commuting the sentence even while he pronounced it. The consequences of sin would be serious—pain in childbirth, relational conflict, toil in work, expulsion from the garden, and, most terrible, death and separation from God. But God would not let sin have the last word.

Even as he concluded his condemning words to the Serpent, God gave a hint at what he planned to do for the human race. He would not leave them without hope. And in these words of hope, we find a pattern for the conflict that will continue until the new creation comes.

While Adam and Eve were listening, God told the Serpent that there would be enmity—or hatred—between the "seed" (or "offspring") of the Serpent and the seed of the woman. But this enmity is not as simple as a rivalry between two sports teams—even an intense rivalry such as the one between the University of Michigan and Ohio State University. I'm a Michigan Wolverine fan, but God has taught me that he can overcome even the biggest rivalry in college sports by continuing to put Ohio State people into my life. I have learned to love them in spite of this glaring weakness. And the "hatred" between Michigan and Ohio State is nothing like the feud between the Hatfields and McCoys, which was a bloody affair that led to the deaths of at least a dozen men from these families. But in spite of the legends about its longevity, even that feud eventually petered out after a few decades.

The enmity between the seed of the Serpent and the seed of the woman would not peter out in a generation or two. It would continue for many generations. Adam and Eve thought that it might end in the second generation. In fact, when their first son, Cain, was born, Eve said, "I have gotten a man with the help of the Lord" (Gen. 4:1). This phrase literally reads, "I have gotten a man, Yahweh." While this phrase is open to interpretation, it is possible to understand it to mean, "I have gotten a man from Yahweh," with the sense being that Eve thought this could be the promised seed who would crush the seed of the Serpent.

But the son of Eve actually proved himself to be more in the line of the Serpent than in the line of the woman. Cain did not crush the head of the Serpent. Instead, he crushed the head of his own brother. It is almost as if the Serpent was trying to turn the words of Genesis 3:15 on their head by having one son of the woman crush the head of the other.

In trying to do that, the Serpent was simply fulfilling the words of Genesis 3:15 for the first of many times. God told the Serpent that as part of the enmity between his line and the line of the woman, he would bruise the heel of the seed of the woman. In an understated irony, the raging attempts of the Serpent to crush the woman's offspring are ultimately just bruises on the heel.

For a brief moment, the Serpent may have thought he had wiped out the line of the woman. But God's promised line would not die so easily. Soon, Adam and Eve had another son, a new seed, Seth (Gen. 4:25), and the line of promise continued through him. But would Seth be the one who would crush the Serpent's head?

If we keep reading in Genesis, it soon becomes obvious that Seth was not the one. And, in fact, we quickly find another serious threat from the seed of the Serpent.

While the family line of Adam and Eve was fulfilling the command to be fruitful and multiply, it seems that most of their descendants were defecting to the line of the Serpent. Like Cain before them, they were running from God's original design and command to represent him as his image bearers in creation. Instead of serving as those who represented God in a fallen world as they waited for him to fulfill the promise of Genesis 3:15, people continued to multiply their wickedness.

As the prophecy of Genesis 3:15 unfolds in the early chapters of the Bible, we can see at least two crucial themes for the rest of redemptive history in action. First, the enmity between the seed of the Serpent and the seed of the woman is very real. From the murder of Abel to the increasing wickedness of the human race, it is clear that the Serpent is serious about contesting God's plan for the offspring of the woman at every turn. Because of this, we can see a second important theme: the Serpent and his seed are committed to doing everything possible to turn God's prophecy around and crush the head of the woman's seed. But the results of these attempts are only a confirmation of the prophecy itself: try as they might, the Serpent and his seed can only bruise the heel of the woman's seed.

But let's not misunderstand what is happening. This is not a yin and yang deal, where everyone is waiting for the seed of the woman to show up and bring balance to the force. The reality is that when God decides to show the seed of the Serpent what he can and will do, the true *imbalance* of power becomes crystal clear in a hurry.

We can see God's sovereign hand in all of this at two places in the early chapters of Genesis. First, when the wickedness of humanity reached a boiling point, God chose to wipe out the entire line of the Serpent in the flood. The only true seed of the woman left were Noah and his family. The seed of the Serpent were decimated and God's righteous judgment was displayed, showing that he is serious about judging sin. We must not forget that God's judgment is coming on those who continue to defy his lordship and authority over them.

But this was not the final, decisive victory of the seed of the woman, because Noah's own son quickly defected to the Serpent's line. By Genesis 11, the Serpent's seed were thriving again. Those of his line were looking to make a name for themselves by building a tower. Once again, however, we see God's sovereign power on display. He brought confusion and chaos as judgment, and so put a halt to their plans for greatness at the Tower of Babel.

You see, all of Genesis 4–11, and indeed all of the rest of the Bible, is really just the outworking of Genesis 3:15. While the enmity between the seed of the woman and the seed of the Serpent was a real and lasting battle, the promise found in this first proclamation of the good news was never really in doubt. In our next chapter, we will meet a man through whom God would continue this promise and clarify his covenant commitment.

KEY BIBLICAL THEOLOGICAL THEMES

Redemption
Seed of the woman

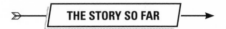

THE STORY SO FAR

God created a kingdom, and he is the King, but he made human beings to represent him in that kingdom. Adam and Eve rejected this call, which led to sin and death. But God promised to defeat the Serpent through the seed of the woman.

ABRAHAM

In you all the families of the
earth shall be blessed.

Genesis 12:2–3

Even while the effects of God's curse on humanity and the conflict between the seed of the Serpent and the seed of the woman raged on, God was working to fulfill the promise of Genesis 3:15—that the seed of the woman would one day crush the Serpent. To this end, he called one man to be the agent through whom he would bring his saving blessings to the world. At the Tower of Babel, the people in the line of the Serpent tried to make a name for themselves (Gen. 11:4), but we will see in the next stop on our tour through the Bible that God's plan was to take one man and make a name for him.

God came to a man named Abram (later changed to Abraham) with an astonishing promise:

> And I will make of you a great nation, and I will bless you and make your name great, so that you will be a blessing. I

will bless those who bless you, and him who dishonors you
I will curse, and in you all the families of the earth shall be
blessed. (Gen. 12:2–3)

Before you start wondering what made Abraham so great,
let's be clear about something—it was not because he was
so righteous or noble that God called him and promised to
make his name great. In fact, he was an idolater, a worshiper
of other gods (Josh. 24:2). There was nothing about Abraham
that made him particularly worthy of God's call.

Unlike the builders of the Tower of Babel, Abraham was
minding his business, not seeking a great name. God did not
decide to make Abraham's name great because he had built a
tower that would bring him fame. Instead, God graciously took
the initiative and made a covenant with Abraham, choosing
him to be the one through whom the offspring of the woman
would come.

God appeared to him and gave him the most amazing
promises—promises that both moved forward the promise
of Genesis 3:15 and gave more details about God's plan of redemption. Because of this, it is important at this point in our
tour through the Bible to stop and look at the promises God
made to Abraham in Genesis 12:2–3. In this amazing text, God
made two spectacular promises: he would make Abraham a
great nation and a great blessing.

When you boil it down, what is needed to make a great
nation or, for that matter, any nation? We could talk about
laws, leaders, and maybe a capable military, and all of those
are probably important ingredients. But for any nation, great
or small, to survive, it needs land and people.

Abraham's problem was that he had neither. First of all, he
was not a homeowner. He was a nomad, a wandering shep-
herd. While his father had probably amassed a certain amount

of wealth in terms of livestock, no amount of cattle could make up for not owning land. But God promised him a land—a place where God would dwell with his people.

Also, Genesis 11:30 mentions that Abraham's wife, Sarai (later changed to Sarah), was barren. While they certainly had plenty of servants, Abraham and Sarah had no children they could name as their heirs. At this point, Abraham was about seventy-five and Sarah was sixty-five—not exactly prime childbearing years. When they died, all of their property would go to another family. But God promised to make Abraham, a landless, childless nomad, into a great nation.

God also promised that Abraham would be a blessing to all the families of the earth. You might think that since he had money, Abraham should have been able to accomplish this one himself. After all, don't we tend to think in terms of finances and prosperity when we think of God's blessing?

Don't tell the guys at Trinity Broadcasting Network, but financial prosperity is not the primary indicator of God's blessing. Think back to the garden. What was the greatest blessing that God gave to Adam and Eve? The greatest blessing was living in God's very presence, knowing him, and worshiping him. So when we think of the promised blessing to Abraham, a big part of it is the very presence of God. Being from an idolatrous family, Abraham was not exactly the best man to mediate the presence of God to the world. Nonetheless, the promise was that through him, all of the families of the earth would receive a blessing. The blessing of God was never intended for a single family or a single nation. It was intended to be worldwide in scope.

So Abraham was a childless, homeless, idolatrous old man. He seemed to be an unlikely candidate to be the one through whom God's promise to crush the head of the Serpent would be fulfilled. In fact, he seemed like a better candidate to carry on the seed of the Serpent than the seed of the woman. But as the story of redemption unfolds, we discover that God often uses unlikely people and unlikely ways to accomplish his purposes. God intervened in amazing ways to overcome the seeming barriers in Abraham's life.

In the days immediately following God's promises in Genesis 12, Abraham and Sarah had plenty of reasons to doubt his word. They grew no younger, and as the years turned into decades, they still did not have a son. At one point, they tried to take matters into their own hands: Sarah convinced Abraham to have a child with her servant Hagar. But God would not be so easily manipulated. It was the son of Abraham and Sarah, not Hagar, who would be the heir of God's covenant promises.

Even as the years rolled by and the couple remained childless, God kept reiterating his promises to them. He changed the name of Abram, which means something like "exalted father," to Abraham, which means "father of a multitude." Sarai's name became Sarah, which means "princess."[3] She would be the mother of a nation.

Finally, twenty-five years after God had appeared to Abraham in Genesis 12, it happened. They had a son named Isaac. It was through this son that God would bring blessing to the world. It was through the offspring of Abraham that God would one day crush the Serpent's head.

But it would take a while. In the rest of Genesis, we meet the rest of Abraham's family. His son Isaac had two sons, Jacob and Esau. It was through Jacob's family that the line of promise continued, and the family tree really started to branch out. Just as God had promised, the family would become a nation.

So in the years following his initial promises in Genesis 12, God laid the foundation for multiplying Abraham's family line and making his descendants a nation. But they still did not have any land. And while God told Abraham that he would give his seed the land from the Nile River to the Euphrates—that is, from modern-day Egypt to Iraq—they would not get it right away. They had to go to Egypt and wait hundreds of years before they would finally get the land. But the promise was secure. God was determined to bless his people in the place he would give them.

The last of the promises that God made to Abraham was the promise to bless all the families of the earth through him. But to be a blessing to others, Abraham had to receive a blessing from God first. And that is exactly what happened. As the promise was unpacked over time, God told Abraham that he would be "their God" (Gen. 17:7–8).

The promise to be their God was not a light thing. With these words, God was promising to give the same blessing to Abraham and his offspring that he gave to Adam and Eve: he would live with them as their God and they as his people. But this raises a question: What would keep Abraham and his seed from messing up the same way Adam and Eve did? How could God guarantee that they wouldn't break this covenant as well?

In Genesis 15, we find an amazing answer to this question. About one year before Isaac was born, God came to Abraham and gave him a strange vision. God asked Abraham to sacrifice several animals and cut the carcasses in half. Then God appeared to him in a vision as a smoking firepot and a flaming torch that passed between the halves of the animals.

While this bizarre scene might be incomprehensible to many today, in the ancient world, its meaning was clear. It was common for two partners who were entering a covenant to sacrifice and divide animals just as Abraham did. They would then walk between the animals together, as a way of saying to each other, "May I be like these animals if I fail to keep this covenant."

But in the vision of Genesis 15, God walked through the divided animals alone. By doing this, he was binding himself to keep both sides of the covenant! He was not only committing to keep the promises himself, but was also committing that if Abraham failed to remain loyal and keep the covenant, he—God!—would suffer the consequences of that failure. God was binding himself to both the promises of Genesis 12:2–3 and the obligations of taking the blessing to all the families of the earth. In this amazing scene, God was binding his own fate with that of Abraham's seed!

In the coming chapters, we will see these promises continue to be fulfilled and multiplied, but the foundation for the rest of what is to come is found in the story of Abraham. It was to Abraham that God clarified that the line of the seed of the woman would run through this family, and it was in the vision to Abraham that God made plain his utter commitment to making these promises happen—so much so that he was willing to put himself on the line.

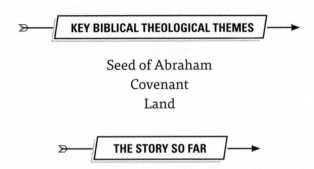

KEY BIBLICAL THEOLOGICAL THEMES

Seed of Abraham
Covenant
Land

THE STORY SO FAR

God created a kingdom, and he is the King, but he made human beings to represent him in that kingdom. Adam and Eve rejected this call, which led to sin and death. But God promised to defeat the Serpent through the seed of the woman, who is also the seed of Abraham. Through Abraham's family, the covenant blessings would come to the world.

JUDAH THE KING

The scepter shall not depart from Judah.

Genesis 49:10

If you've read C. S. Lewis's Chronicles of Narnia books, you know that one of the persistent themes in the series is that, as Trufflehunter the badger says, "Narnia was never right except when a Son of Adam was king."[4] Whether it was Peter, Susan, Edmund, and Lucy, or Caspian's dynasty, Narnia's best days were under the reign of Adam's descendants. I think that Lewis understood something about the image of God and the commission of Adam and Eve.

While Lewis was writing about a world filled with talking beasts and walking trees, this theme is actually truer in the real world than it is in Narnia. In Narnia, the highest King was Aslan the lion. But in the real world, the promised King is a true son of Adam, a son of Abraham, and, as we will see in this chapter, a son of Judah.

Throughout the Bible, we hear a lot about God's promises to Abraham, Isaac, and Jacob—often called the patriarchs.

His covenant with them carried forward the promise that he made to Adam and Eve in the garden and was the way in which he planned to bring the blessing of his presence back to the world. While other covenants would be introduced, they would build on each other as God worked to fulfill his promises to Abraham.

But when we look at the behavior of the patriarchs, we don't exactly see an exemplary track record. Not much about them would lead us to believe that they would be instrumental in God's redemptive purposes for the world.

Abraham lied about being married to Sarah and put her in danger of being raped—twice. His son Isaac followed in his father's footsteps, denying that he was married to his wife, Rebekah, to save his own skin. Isaac's son Jacob manipulated his father and his brother, Esau, in order to get a bigger inheritance. But then Esau threatened to kill Jacob, so Jacob had to live in exile for decades. While he was in exile, he married two sisters because their father tricked him into marrying a different sister than the one he loved. From those two wives, along with their servants, Jacob had twelve sons. But he loved his eleventh son, Joseph, the most, which led Joseph's brothers to sell him into slavery and tell their dad that he was dead. And that's only part of the story!

Even in the midst of all of this dysfunction, God was working to preserve the promised line. And this teaches us that God's saving purposes ultimately do not hang on any mere man. As he promised Abraham, God would take on the weight of both sides of his covenant—but still, he pledged himself to work out his promises through the family line of Abraham.

If you have read the book of Genesis, you know that Joseph plays an important role in the last part of the book. The promise to Abraham's family is the reason why Joseph has such a role. God used Joseph to preserve Abraham's line, the line of promise. Through God's providence, Joseph ascended to the rank of second-in-command in Egypt. Through God's wisdom, Joseph prepared the population of the entire region—including his brothers—to face a seven-year-long famine. When the brothers came to buy the grain Joseph had stored away, Joseph was reconciled to his family, and his father, along with all of his brothers, came to live with him in Egypt. So Joseph's life was not about a Technicolor dreamcoat, and it was not even about Joseph's moral fiber (though this was certainly important). No, the story of Joseph was about God's promise to preserve his people, even in the face of seeming death. While the line of the Serpent was trying to snuff out the line of Abraham, God preserved Joseph so that he could preserve his brothers.

As we round the bend to our next text, Genesis 49:10, we will see that, while God used Joseph to save the family from famine and death, he chose another brother to lay the foundation for a royal dynasty. Adam and Eve were created to help manage God's kingdom and rule on his behalf. In a way, they were supposed to be a king and queen. So we should not be surprised to find God making royal promises.

When Jacob, Abraham's grandson, lay on his deathbed in Egypt, he blessed each of his sons in different ways. But when he came to Judah, he gave a royal blessing:

> The scepter shall not depart from Judah,
>   nor the ruler's staff from between his feet,
> until tribute comes to him;
>   and to him shall be the obedience of the peoples.
>   (Gen. 49:10)

If you had to pick one of Jacob's sons to be the father of a king, who would you choose? Joseph would probably be your first selection. After that, you might pick Reuben, because he was the oldest. It might take you awhile to land on Judah.

Most of what we know about Judah is pretty rough. The first time we hear Judah speak is when Joseph's brothers threw him in a pit and then tried to decide what to do with him. Judah suggested that, instead of killing Joseph, they could both get rid of him and make a little money at the same time by selling him into slavery (Gen. 37:26–27). It only got worse from there. While Joseph languished in Egypt, Judah's first son died without children. As was the custom, Judah's second son married his brother's widow, but he too died childless. Instead of letting Tamar, his daughter-in-law, marry his third son to carry on the family line, Judah sent her away. But Tamar tricked Judah himself into sleeping with her, and she had his twin sons. So he was both father and grandfather to his grandsons. It would be hard to make this kind of thing up!

It was to this broken family line that God promised the scepter of kingship, the ruler's staff. But the descendent of Judah would not only be the king of Israel, he would also be a king over the nations. Jacob prophesied that tribute and the obedience of the nations would come to the royal son of Judah—an amazing promise to make to such a man.

These promises about the nations should not catch us completely off guard. Remember the promise to Abraham: "in you all the families of the earth shall be blessed." If it was God's intention to restore and even expand the commission of Adam and Eve to help him rule his worldwide kingdom—and it was—then we would expect that the blessing of Abraham would go to the nations through a royal descendent of Abraham. That is exactly what was happening here. A descendent of Abraham—and more specifically, as this text reveals to us, a descendent of Judah—would not only bless the nations, but in doing so, he also would renew and even expand God's kingdom presence in this world.

So in Genesis 49, we discover that the seed of Abraham is

also a royal seed, a king through whom the nations will be blessed. As we look back on the way that God preserved his people through Joseph and even used the upside-down actions of Judah to preserve the line of promise, we can see his relentless commitment to keeping his saving promises.

In Genesis, we learn that the seed of the woman, the promised seed of Abraham, and the royal seed of Judah will be the agent through whom God will fulfill his commitment to crush the head of the Serpent. But at the end of this first book in the Bible, the seed of Abraham, the Promised One, has not finally and fully fulfilled God's promises—at least not yet.

You may be wondering at this point if this book is deceptively titled. After all, we are already a third of the way done, and we still haven't made it out of Genesis! Let me assure you that this is intentional. Our goal is to walk through the storyline of the Bible by looking at just a few key texts. To grasp the basic storyline of the Bible, however, we have to get a clear understanding of the beginning. In fact, there are many more parts of Genesis we could and perhaps should examine. We haven't spent time on the flood, the land promises, or the hints about sacrifices that we see in the stories of Cain and Abel, Noah, and Abraham. But we have seen the basic covenant structure in Genesis, and this is the foundation for the rest of the Bible's storyline and, in fact, the rest of history.

Now we will pick up our pace and move past many key themes far too quickly. In our next chapter, we will turn our attention to how the sacrifices and the law of Moses move the story of the Bible and the saving promises forward.

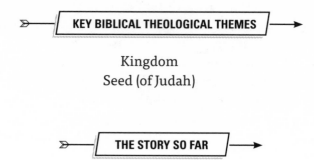

KEY BIBLICAL THEOLOGICAL THEMES

Kingdom
Seed (of Judah)

THE STORY SO FAR

God created a kingdom, and he is the King, but he made human beings to represent him in that kingdom. Adam and Eve rejected this call, which led to sin and death. But God promised to defeat the Serpent through the seed of the woman, who is also the seed of Abraham. Through Abraham's family, and specifically Judah's royal seed, the covenant blessings would come to the world.

THE **PASSOVER LAMB**

The LORD will pass over the door.

Exodus 12:23

"Why is all that bloody stuff in the Bible? Couldn't God have just skipped past the law, with its sacrifices and weird regulations, to go straight to the good news?"

If you have ever asked yourself these questions, you weren't the first. Many Christians struggle to understand why the law of Moses was necessary. While I might not be able to answer all of your questions in a book of this size, in this chapter I want to focus on the law, and especially its sacrifices, by focusing on the Passover in Exodus 12. But to get to this text, we need to fast-forward about 430 years from our last stop. As I said in the last chapter, it's time to pick up the pace a bit!

At the beginning of Exodus, we discover that Abraham's family is actually farther away from living in God's place and extending the blessing to the nations than when we left off. After Abraham's family went down to Egypt in the time of Joseph, they settled there and started to multiply. During the next four centuries, they grew from the seventy-person family that Jacob led down from Palestine into a nation of around two million people, who became known as the Israelites, after a new name that God gave to Jacob—Israel. Unsurprisingly, the Egyptians saw them as a threat—especially after a new royal dynasty that didn't know Joseph came to power. So the Egyptians enslaved the family of Abraham and forced them into hard labor. They still were not in God's Promised Land, and they were under the oppression of the Egyptians. The fact is, they needed to be rescued!

The seed of the Serpent, here embodied by the Egyptians, was rising up to try to extinguish God's promised line. To slow the growth of Abraham's family, Egypt's king, the pharaoh, commanded that all of the Israelites' baby boys be killed. But one child escaped this fate. Moses was rescued, raised in Pharaoh's court, and eventually called to lead God's people out of slavery (after some trials along the way).

God heard the groaning of his people and, Exodus 2:24 tells us, he "remembered his covenant with Abraham, with Isaac, and with Jacob." He had pledged to keep his covenant with the patriarchs, and he would take the next step in doing that by bringing his people out of slavery and giving them the law. So whatever else we might say about the law and its commandments, we cannot forget that it is a continuation of God's promises to Abraham, which are actually a continuation of his saving promise to Adam and Eve.

How exactly did God rescue his people from slavery in Egypt? While he showed his power to the Egyptians in ten plagues, we find the main answer to this question in Exodus 12, where the final plague, the death of all the firstborn in Egypt, is recounted. On the night before he would finally rescue them from Egypt, God commanded each Israelite family to sacrifice a lamb and spread its blood over the top of their door and the doorposts on each side. Then he said:

> For the LORD will pass through to strike the Egyptians, and when he sees the blood on the lintel and on the two doorposts, the LORD will pass over the door and will not allow the destroyer to enter your houses to strike you. (Ex. 12:23)

In a very direct way, God rescued his people with the blood of the Passover lambs. Because the lambs were sacrificed, the people did not have to die. Because the blood of the lambs was spilt, the firstborn sons in Abraham's family were safe.

It had to be this way because the Egyptians were not the only ones under a death sentence. The Israelites were just as guilty, if not more so. While the Egyptians were guilty of worshiping lots of other gods, the Israelites were guilty both of idolatry and of doubting God's promises to save them.[5] They quickly doubted God's promises after Pharaoh increased their workload (Ex. 5:21). Even after God had delivered them from Egypt, they continued to doubt him at the Red Sea, at Mount Sinai, and in the wilderness. Like Adam and Eve, they doubted that God's words were true. And because of that, like Adam and Eve, they were under a death sentence. But when God judged Egypt, he provided a way of escape for his people. And this way of escape laid the foundation for the law he was about to give them.

As the Lord was passing through Egypt, striking down all of the firstborn sons, he passed over the houses that were marked with the blood of the lambs. The lambs died so that the firstborn sons would not. Although we saw hints of it before, this is one of the earliest clear examples of the important biblical principle of substitution. The Passover lambs were substitutes for the firstborn in Israel. In this first Passover, God considered the sacrifices of lambs to be sufficient to save his people from judgment—at least for the moment.

But there was also a big problem with this sacrifice: the people soon would need another one. As we saw a moment ago, the people had sinned repeatedly in the past, and it would not take them long to sin again, and again, and again. In order to point the Israelites to their constant failure to trust that God's words are true and their constant need of forgiveness, he gave them the law.

After bringing them through the Red Sea and to the foot of Mount Sinai, God continued to provide a way of escape. He gave the Israelites a law that organized them into a nation and taught them about his holiness and what he demands of his people. He gave them a covenant filled with stipulations and rules, but that covenant was built on both his previous promises to Abraham and his gracious work to free them from slavery in Egypt.

So the law set Israel apart as a nation, as God's "treasured possession" (Deut. 7:6). But the backbone of the law was the sacrificial system. Every year, the Levite priests, descendants of Jacob's son Levi, needed to offer hundreds and hundreds of sacrifices. If they were keeping the commandments of the law, every descendent of Abraham would see the animal sacrifices. The message sent to each of them by every bull and goat sacrificed was: "You deserve this. This should be your blood."

Every year, the nation would celebrate the anniversary of that first Passover in Egypt. Every year, each family was to sacrifice another lamb as a substitute. Now put yourself in the place of an Israelite for a moment. If you were truly grasping the message of the sacrifices, you would think: "The consequence of sin is death, but in the garden, God promised to overcome the effects of sin and finally defeat the Serpent. However, these sacrifices have to be repeated year after year.

So they can't actually be defeating sin. In fact, when I offer a sacrifice, I am admitting that I deserve death. So unless something or someone greater comes, all I am doing is delaying the inevitable. I need a greater sacrifice!"

While God had many purposes for the law, one of the clearest and most important was to point to the need for a greater sacrifice still to come. This sacrifice would have to defeat the Serpent and reverse the effects of God's curse. So we have to conclude that the promised seed would somehow defeat sin by providing a final and complete sacrifice.

God *redeemed* his people from slavery in Egypt by means of a *substitute*. Very early in the Bible, then, the patterns of redemption are established. In the first Passover, we see the pattern that God established in the law. The entire Mosaic covenant points forward to the need for a greater sacrifice. It points us to the promised seed.

After the newly constituted nation of Israel left Sinai, they wandered in the desert for forty years because of their ongoing sin—time and time again, they succumbed to temptations in the wilderness. But God in his grace eventually led them into the Promised Land. God gave Israel victory over the nations occupying the land so that Moses's successor, Joshua, eventually could tell them, "Not one word has failed of all the good things that the LORD your God promised concerning you" (Josh. 23:14).

At this point in the story, it might seem that God finally was restoring those garden-like conditions. The Israelites had God's direct revelation through the law to rule them and God's blessing with his presence among them. And he had brought his people into the land that he had promised them. But like Adam and Eve, they continued to doubt God's word, to defy his law, and to desire to live apart from his presence. Like Adam and Eve, they were not satisfied with God's rule over them.

Eventually, they asked for a king like those in the nations around them.

Believe it or not, that is exactly what God gave them. But this was not the kind of king who would be able to finally lead the defeat of sin and death they should have been looking for. Instead, King Saul was exactly what they wanted—a king like the ones in the surrounding nations, a king who relied on military strength, the wisdom of man, and the worship of false gods.

But this was not the King through whom God's promises would come. That King would come much later.

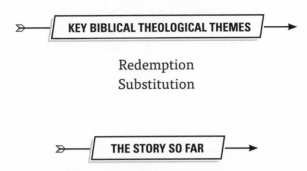

KEY BIBLICAL THEOLOGICAL THEMES

Redemption
Substitution

THE STORY SO FAR

God created a kingdom, and he is the King, but he made human beings to represent him in that kingdom. Adam and Eve rejected this call, which led to sin and death. But God promised to defeat the Serpent through the seed of the woman, who is also the seed of Abraham. Through Abraham's family, and specifically Judah's royal seed, the covenant blessings would come to the world. Because all people were guilty and deserved death, the sacrifices of the Mosaic law revealed more clearly their need for a substitute.

KING DAVID

I will establish the throne of his kingdom forever.

2 Samuel 7:12–13

Apart from Johnny Cash and a few others, I am not a big fan of country singers. Don't get me wrong, I don't have anything against the genre, but most modern country music seems about the same as most pop music these days—lots of flash without much substance.

But I did grow up hearing some country music, and a line in one Garth Brooks song stands out in my mind: "Sometimes I thank God for unanswered prayers." After that line, the theology of the song goes downhill pretty quickly, and the reality is that Brooks is not talking about unanswered prayers, but about prayers that God did not answer in the way he wanted. But I know what he means—at least, I think I know what he means. If God gave us everything we asked for, we would be miserable. In his mercy, he often doesn't let our lives unfold the way we want.

In the same way, God does not let anyone—even King

David—dictate the unfolding of his redemptive plan. As we will see in our next stop, God is committed to accomplishing his purposes in his way, and neither sinful human ambition nor a misguided desire to "help God out" can change that.

A few stops back, we saw sinful ambition turned on its head when God thwarted the builders of the Tower of Babel, who were trying to make a name for themselves. Instead, he promised to make Abraham's name great. In the next stop on our tour of the storyline of the Bible, we will see him turn David's godly ambition to build a house for God into an astonishing promise to build a house and make a name for David!

It didn't take long for the prophet Samuel to see that Israel's first king, Saul, was not the Promised One the family of Abraham had been awaiting so long. But this shouldn't have surprised anyone who was paying attention at this point. After all, Saul was from the "tribe" of Jacob's son Benjamin, not Judah (the extended families of the twelve sons of Jacob became the twelve "tribes" that made up the nation of Israel). The promised seed of the woman had to be not just the seed of Abraham, but also the seed of Judah.

As King Saul's short-lived dynasty spiraled downward, God sent Samuel to the house of Jesse in the family of Judah. There he found Jesse's youngest son, secretly anointed him to be the next king, and then left young David to wait. As the months passed, David began to resemble the king for whom many in Israel had been waiting. He famously defeated the giant Goliath, along with many more of God's enemies. As he fought for the people of God, winning victory after victory, Saul could see which way the wind was blowing, and he eventually sought to kill David. But God preserved David and kept giving him victories. When Saul and all his sons except one died on the battlefield, David finally became king.

During the first seven or so years of David's reign, he

consolidated his power and conquered Jerusalem, making it his capital. As he established his seat of power in the city, he wanted to replace the tent that had been used for worship since the days of the exodus with a lasting temple to honor God and give the people a permanent place of worship. He had the ark of the covenant, the very place where God had promised to meet with his people (Ex. 25:22), and was ready to bring it into the new temple. As we can see in the Psalms, David walked closely with God and understood what it meant to enjoy the blessing of God's presence!

From everything we can tell, David's desire was a noble one. After all, what was the great covenant blessing that Adam and Eve lost in the garden but God promised to restore? It was that God himself would live with his people—that his presence would be with them forever. And what better way to facilitate this than by building a permanent house for God to dwell in so that his people could properly worship and sacrifice to him? David even asked for the approval of the prophet Nathan. Nathan gave him the go-ahead, going so far as to say, "the Lord is with you" (2 Sam. 7:3).

But God had a different plan. While David may have been thinking about building a house where the people in Israel could worship, God was thinking of a house where all nations might worship. While David may have been thinking about a place for God's presence to dwell in Jerusalem, God was thinking of a much larger house where he would dwell, and where David's line would reign forever. In other words, God came to David with a much bigger promise than he could ever have imagined.

God told Nathan that he needed to go set the king straight. David would not be the one to build the temple. In the four centuries since he had given the law, God had not demanded that the people build him a house. And David would not be the one to do it either. That project would be reserved for his son. But while David was not going to build a house for God, God would build a house for David (2 Sam. 7:11).

So we finally arrive at our next stop on our tour through the Bible, where God explained what the house that he was building for David would look like. It would not be a house of cedar wood, such as David wanted to build. Instead, this house would be a royal dynasty that would last forever!

> When your days are fulfilled and you lie down with your fathers, I will raise up your offspring after you, who shall come from your body, and I will establish his kingdom. He shall build a house for my name, and I will establish the throne of his kingdom forever. (2 Sam. 7:12–13)

God told David that after he died, his royal line would continue. God would establish the kingdom of David's son forever. But there was more to the promise than that. Not only would God establish the kingdom of David's son, but this son would also fulfill David's ambition by building a house for God. As he built this temple, the king, David's son, would be the one who would bring the blessing of God's presence to his people in a lasting way.

As we step back and put together some of the pieces of the story that we have already seen, we can't miss this theme. As we saw earlier, the very presence of God was a big part of the promised blessing of Abraham. Do you see the connection? The royal offspring would bring the blessing promised to Abraham. The line of David would bring the presence of God to the nations!

It shouldn't surprise us that when Solomon, David's son, finally finished building the temple, he called it the place where "all the peoples of the earth may know that the LORD is God; there is no other" (1 Kings 8:60). The temple was the place where the blessing of God's presence would go to all the families of the earth and where the royal seed of Judah would fulfill his commission to receive tribute from the nations.

So was Solomon the seed of the woman, the seed of Abraham, and the royal seed of Judah? You might think so from reading the last part of the promise: "I will establish the throne of his kingdom forever." Maybe David or other careful readers of the law of Moses thought that Solomon could be the one to reverse the curse of sin and death and actually reign forever. In fact, God told David, "I will be to him a father, and he shall be to me a son" (2 Sam. 7:14). This is intimate language—the kind God uses for few others.

If we keep reading in this verse, however, we see that this covenant that God was making with David had certain conditions. He told David that if this royal son was unfaithful, then God would "discipline him with the rod of men" (2 Sam. 7:14). Unfortunately, that is exactly what happened to Solomon. As he grew in wealth and power, his heart drifted away from God. And so the promised discipline came. Neither David nor Solomon was the promised descendant of Judah. In fact, because of Solomon's disobedience, his son Rehoboam reigned only over the tribes of Judah and Benjamin. The other tribes broke away and formed a kingdom in the north.

Things just went south from there. The same problem kept king after king from finally and fully doing what a king ought to do. Because of idolatry, foolishness, and pride, none of the kings of Judah or Israel in the north could keep the terms of God's covenant with David. They were all unfaithful, and just as God had promised David, they all faced the discipline of men.

As the years rolled by and the kings got worse, they led the people of God further and further away from the blessing of God. The people needed a faithful king who could keep the law of God perfectly. So it seemed that until the problem of sin was finally fully solved, the promises to David and, for that matter, the promises to Adam, Abraham, and Judah could not be fulfilled. The people of God still needed a substitute who would solve the problem of sin once and for all.

KEY BIBLICAL THEOLOGICAL THEMES

Kingdom
Offspring (seed) of David
Covenant

THE STORY SO FAR

God created a kingdom, and he is the King, but he made human beings to represent him in that kingdom. Adam and Eve rejected this call, which led to sin and death. But God promised to defeat the Serpent through the seed of the woman, who is also the seed of Abraham. Through Abraham's family, and specifically Judah's royal seed, David, the covenant blessings would come to the world. Because all people were guilty and deserved death, the sacrifices of the Mosaic law revealed more clearly their need for a substitute.

THE SUFFERING SERVANT

The LORD has laid on him the iniquity of us all.

Isaiah 53:6

At this point in our story, it might seem that we are stuck between a rock and a hard place. A couple of chapters back, we saw the need for the Passover lambs and the sacrifices required by the Mosaic law. In our quick overview of the covenant with David and the failure of any king to obey perfectly, we saw that those sacrifices were needed as much as ever. But it also seemed that those sacrifices were not solving the problem. The cloud of sin continued to loom large over Israel, as well as the surrounding nations. The Philistines, the Moabites, the Assyrians, and the Babylonians, to mention a few, kept leading Judah, Israel, and their kings away from faithfulness to God. The kings of Judah and Israel continued to lead the people deeper and deeper into idolatry. The people still needed the sacrifices, but the sacrifices were not solving the problem! Something had to give.

Not only did the kings of Judah in the south and Israel in

the north continue to sin, turn their backs on God, and lead the people astray, but they also stopped following the very instructions that God had given them to address their sin in the law of Moses. Soon after the ten tribes in the north broke away from Judah, King Jeroboam built two idolatrous altars: one at Dan in the northern part of the nation and one at Bethel in the south. He was afraid that if his subjects continued to offer sacrifices and visit the temple in Jerusalem as God had commanded, their loyalty would soon swing back to the kings of Judah. In short, he chose political power over fidelity to God. But that never happens anymore, does it?

Surely the kings of Judah did better, you must be thinking. After all, the temple was right in their backyard, and they had the priests around them all the time. But the sad reality is that the kings of Judah hardly did any better when it came to keeping the law. While we don't know all of the details of what they did and did not do, at minimum, Judah failed to keep the Sabbath regulations God gave for the land (Lev. 25:8–22) at least seventy times (2 Chron. 36:21). Since they were required to let the land rest once every seven years, this is 490 years of disobedience!

And it was not just the Sabbath instructions they failed to keep. For at least a couple of centuries, they didn't even have the entire law, let alone keep it! When Josiah was king, more than three hundred years after David died, he commissioned a series of renovations to the temple. While working on this project, the priests found the lost "Book of the Law" and read it aloud to the people. As near as we can tell, the last time they had heard the law read in public was during the reign of Jehoshaphat—about 250 years earlier. Imagine if the American Declaration of Independence had been read on July 4, 1776, and then lost until today (by the way, history nerds, yes, I know that it was not actually read aloud on that day). This would be about the same amount of time that elapsed in Israel between public readings of the law.

It's not as if God's people were trying and failing to keep the law. No, they were not trying at all, because they did not even have it! They still needed sacrifices and substitutes for their sins, and neglecting the sacrificial system only made things worse.

Because they did not keep the law, God's judgment came on them, just as it always does when a covenant is broken. Assyria conquered Israel in the north in about 722 BC. Two hundred and fifty years later, the Babylonians conquered Judah and led the people into captivity, where they remained for about seventy years.

But it is not as if when the Israelites tried to keep the law, they finally got rid of sin. After they returned from their exile in Babylon, the people were fairly committed to trying to obey the law—at least, as they interpreted it. But the law and its sacrifices were still not enough to remove sin once and for all. The people still needed a long-term solution.

Now, all of that background finally brings us to our next stop on our tour through the Bible. About 150 years before Judah went into exile, God gave the prophet Isaiah a vision that pointed forward to the definitive solution to the sin problem. Even in our little survey, it doesn't take long to realize that both Israel and the surrounding nations had sinned. Like lost sheep, they had gone astray—even as we have. Therefore, to finally defeat sin, God would not send an animal sacrifice. Instead, he would send a suffering servant, and the Lord would lay on this servant the iniquity of all his people:

> All we like sheep have gone astray;
>   we have turned—every one—to his own way;

and the LORD has laid on him
the iniquity of us all. (Isa. 53:6)

Many Christians know that Isaiah 53 is often called the "suffering servant chapter," but what many do not know is that this servant shows up often in this part of Isaiah. Chapter 49 is particularly helpful for our understanding of who the servant is. At the beginning of Isaiah 49, God says, "You are my servant, Israel" (v. 3). So it's pretty clear that the nation as a whole is the servant, right?

But keep reading. In verse 5, God says the servant will "bring Jacob back to him . . . that Israel might be gathered to him." So here it seems that the servant is someone else who will bring the nation as a whole back to God. Which is it?

Even the most hardened biblical critic has to admit that this can't be explained away as a simple contradiction. It would take a lot of hubris to say that Isaiah missed this one. I think there is a much better and much simpler solution. Even though we think very individualistically in the modern world, especially in the West, I still think even we can understand what is going on here. We have to set aside our individualism and realize that the biblical writers had a much larger view of the role of the community.

If I were to tell you that His Majesty King George III was not happy with the actions of certain American colonists who dumped a bunch of tea into Boston Harbor in 1773, I would be saying that George himself was displeased. But I could also be saying that the entire British Empire was not happy with the colonists. This is because King George was a symbol for the nation he ruled. Although his power might have been less than that of his predecessors because of constitutional reforms, his actions, his decisions, and his will were the nation's. The individual named George *represented* the British Empire.

The servant in Isaiah acts in a similar way. In verse 3, God can say that Israel is the servant because, in verse 5, the servant is shown to be the single representative of the nation. The servant can say, "I am Israel," in the same kind of way that King Louis XIV of France could say, "I am the state."

If we go back to Isaiah 53 now and unpack verse 6, I think we will have a better understanding of the way this prophecy fits into our story. As we walk through this chapter, we get a stark picture of the horrible task that God set before the servant. He was to be "despised and rejected by men; a man of sorrows, and acquainted with grief" (v. 3). It was his calling to be "stricken, smitten by God, and afflicted" (v. 4). But in verse 5, we discover where this was heading: "upon him was the chastisement that brought us peace, and with his wounds we are healed."

If we go all the way back to God's covenant with Abraham, and then look at the other two major covenants that are built on it, we see that something was always required on the human side. Abraham, Israel, and David all had to keep certain conditions. But they and their descendants all failed to keep the conditions perfectly, so they all had to deal with God's judgment. The sacrifices of the law helped them see what was necessary to escape that judgment—a substitute. But the sacrifices themselves were never enough.

Back in Isaiah 53, all of the covenant penalties come to a head in verse 6: "the LORD has laid on him the iniquity of us all." So here it is: the suffering of the servant as the representative of God's people turns out to be a *substitutionary* suffering. He would take the punishment that they deserved. Also, look at verse 10. It tells us that he would make "an offering for guilt." As the representative of the nation, he would step in and do what all of the sacrifices could never do. He would bring peace and healing. He would absorb the sin and guilt of the nation. He would bear the sin of many (v. 12).

If the suffering servant was one man who represented the entire nation, and his role was to finally and fully deal with the problem of sin and guilt, then he sounds a lot like the seed of the woman from way back in Genesis 3. After all, when you boil it down, the seed's job was to reverse the effects of the fall. The problem that the fall brought was the problem of sin and guilt. So it seems that Isaiah's prophecy connects very closely with the seed promises. Maybe, just maybe, the seed of the woman, the seed of Abraham, and the seed of Judah were all one and the same with the suffering servant. If so, then the Mosaic law and its sacrifices were reminders that when the seed finally came, he would take the covenant penalty on himself and remove sin once and for all.

But there is one problem with this picture. To reverse the effects of the curse, it was not just sin that needed to be defeated. Death was still the great enemy lurking in the background. And it seems that for the seed/servant to complete his mission, death needed to be vanquished as well. That problem leads us to our next stop in Ezekiel 37.

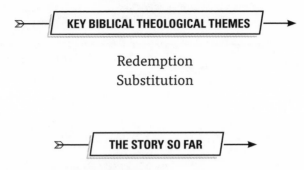

KEY BIBLICAL THEOLOGICAL THEMES

Redemption
Substitution

THE STORY SO FAR

God created a kingdom, and he is the King, but he made human beings to represent him in that kingdom. Adam and Eve rejected this call, which led to sin and death. But God promised to defeat the Serpent through the seed of the woman, who is also the seed of Abraham. Through Abraham's family, and specifically Judah's royal seed, David, the covenant blessings would come to the world. Because all people were guilty and deserved death, the sacrifices of the Mosaic law revealed more clearly their need for a substitute—the suffering servant.

RESURRECTION PROMISED

Can these bones live?

Ezekiel 37:3–5

Some people like to take cross-country trips to see the sights and stop at the tourist attractions along the way. I am not that way. When I take a road trip, my goal is to get from point A to point B as quickly as possible. I went to college in northeastern Wisconsin after growing up about five hundred miles away in southeastern Michigan. Every time my friends and I would make that journey, we wanted to get from Dunbar, Wisconsin, to Woodhaven, Michigan, as quickly as possible. We were always trying to beat the last trip's time. Even though we often talked about stopping at the tourist traps we passed, the lure of Sea Shell City or the World's Largest Crucifix was never quite enough to convince us to actually take the time.

Sometimes, however, a pit stop actually makes your trip quicker and more efficient. If you don't stop for gas, walking a mile each way from your car to the station will slow down your trip. Sometimes a detour is necessary.

So in our tour through the Bible, we are going to take a little detour. We are on our way to Ezekiel 37 to understand the next step in the defeat of sin and death. At this point, we have seen God's covenants with Adam (and Noah), with Abraham, with the nation of Israel in the law, and with David. But there is one more covenant in the Old Testament that we need to look at so that we can understand Ezekiel's prophecy.

Jeremiah is sometimes called the "Weeping Prophet" because, during his ministry, Babylon conquered the kingdom of Judah and took many of its citizens captive. But Jeremiah's message was not all doom and gloom. A remarkable ray of hope broke through the shadows of captivity when God gave him the prophecy of the "new covenant."

In that dark time, God told the people, "Behold, the days are coming, declares the LORD, when I will make a new covenant with the house of Israel and the house of Judah" (Jer. 31:31). God promised to make a new covenant that would build on the previous covenants—and, ultimately, be the way that he would fulfill them all. He went on to unpack this covenant: "I will put my law within them, and I will write it on their hearts. And I will be their God, and they shall be my people. . . . They shall all know me, from the least of them to the greatest, declares the LORD. For I will forgive their iniquity, and I will remember their sin no more" (vv. 33–34).

In short, God was saying he would finally bring the blessing of Abraham, the blessing lost at the fall, by giving his people new hearts and forgiving all of their sins. God would dwell among his people, and the effects of sin would be no more. We saw in the previous chapter that the suffering servant would remove their sin. Then, Jeremiah's prophecy tells us, when he removed sin, a new covenant would be established whereby God would finally dwell with his people.

But we still have one problem—what about death? The

blessing of God's presence in this life is good, but death is still lurking around the corner, waiting to snuff out that blessing. While we see hints at new life in Isaiah 53 and even Jeremiah 31, we need to get back on our main path and move on to our next key text, Ezekiel 37:3–5, to find a fuller answer to the question of how God would overcome death. But keep this new covenant and its promises in mind.

Around the same time that God gave his new covenant promises to Jeremiah, he came to Ezekiel with a series of amazing visions. One of the most vivid pictures in Ezekiel's prophecy, and maybe in the entire Bible, is the vision of the dry bones in Ezekiel 37. These amazing prophecies help us see how God planned to overcome death on the other side of the suffering servant's substitutionary sacrifice:

> And he said to me, "Son of man, can these bones live?" And I answered, "O Lord GOD, you know." Then he said to me, "Prophesy over these bones, and say to them, O dry bones, hear the word of the LORD. Thus says the Lord GOD to these bones: Behold, I will cause breath to enter you, and you shall live." (Ezek. 37:3–5)

At the time when God gave Ezekiel this vision, not many in Judah were optimistic about the future. They were saying, "Our bones are dried up, and our hope is lost; we are indeed cut off" (v. 11). In the aftermath of the devastation that Babylon had brought to the nation, it was hard to see much hope. Few if any families had escaped death and suffering, and the nation itself had lost its independence and hope. The idea of the seed of Abraham crushing the Serpent and bringing the blessing of God to the nations seemed a long way off.

God brought Ezekiel to a valley filled with dry bones, bleached by the sun. Then he asked the prophet the most amazing question: "Can these bones live?" (v. 3). If you were to come across the grisly sight of piles and piles of dried bones, it probably would not cross your mind to wonder whether those bones could live. You would just want to bury them and forget that you ever saw them. Ezekiel cautiously answered, "O Lord GOD, you know." After all, he was talking to the giver of life. But he could not imagine what would happen next.

God commanded Ezekiel to speak to these dried, dusty bones and say: "O dry bones, hear the word of the LORD. Thus says the Lord GOD to these bones: Behold, I will cause breath to enter you, and you shall live" (vv. 4–5). Not only would breath enter the bones, he went on to say, but sinew, flesh, and skin would cover them. God said they would truly live!

So Ezekiel stood over the bones and said what God had told him to say. Immediately, the bones came together and were covered with flesh and skin. This hopeless valley filled with dry bones suddenly became a witness to the power of God's word. Remember what we saw at the beginning of our journey? God speaks, and things happen. God's words give life.

After Ezekiel spoke, those dead and dry bones were whole again, but they still were not alive. So God commanded Ezekiel to tell the "breath," or "spirit," to come and enter the dead. When it did, they came to life and stood on their feet. Don't miss this—when the spirit from God entered them, the dry bones lived. The picture could not be clearer. The Spirit of God gives life—both in the first creation and also here, in his new creation.

Just in case the people had not picked up on the meaning of this vision yet, God told Ezekiel to explain what it symbolized: "Behold, I will open your graves and raise you from your graves, O my people. And I will bring you into the land of Israel. And you shall know that I am the LORD, when I open your graves, and raise you from your graves, O my people. And I will put my Spirit within you, and you shall live, and I will place you in your own land. Then you shall know that I am the LORD" (vv. 12–14). The meaning of the vision was that God would not abandon his people to death. He would, by his Spirit, one day defeat death and bring them into the land that he had promised them. This would be a reversal of the curse. Once again, God would live with his people in the land he gave to them!

If we take a step back, we can see how the prophecies we've looked at in the last two chapters fit together. Hang with me, because this might take a couple of readings to process.

Remember, the goal all along has been the same. God said he would crush the head of the Serpent through the promised offspring of the woman. But to do this, he needed to defeat sin and death. Through the substitutionary sacrifice of the suffering servant, the sin debt of God's people would be paid. He would be the final and complete sacrifice. In the new covenant, God promised to forgive all of his people and to put "the law on their hearts." Sin would be defeated through the servant's sacrifice. God was promising an amazing victory! Once sin was defeated, death's power would die with it. It would no longer hold people captive.

Then God would send his Spirit to give life to his people. It only stands to reason that the first and primary way this would happen was that he would give life to the servant, the representative of God's people. So the promise of Ezekiel 37 was that once sin was defeated, the power of death would be removed. And once the power of death was removed, God's Spirit would have free rein to give life—first to the servant, and then to all those who receive the forgiveness of sin promised in the new covenant and won by the servant's death. Through this vision in Ezekiel 37, God was promising a new creation!

In the prophets, we see the way God would finally defeat the Serpent through the seed of the woman—who must also be the suffering servant. The wisdom of God unpacked as we wind our way through this plan of redemption in the Old Testament is remarkable.

But we are not quite done with the Old Testament yet. We have one more stop that will point us forward to what is to come.

KEY BIBLICAL THEOLOGICAL THEMES

New covenant
Spirit
New creation

THE STORY SO FAR

God created a kingdom, and he is the King, but he made human beings to represent him in that kingdom. Adam and Eve rejected this call, which led to sin and death. But God promised to defeat the Serpent through the seed of the woman, who is also the seed of Abraham. Through Abraham's family, and specifically Judah's royal seed, David, the covenant blessings would come to the world. Because all people were guilty and deserved death, the sacrifices of the Mosaic law revealed more clearly their need for a substitute—the suffering servant. Through the servant and the work of the Spirit, God would establish a new covenant and give lasting life to his people.

NEW CREATION

I create new heavens and a new earth.

Isaiah 65:17

I love to read. While I try to read many kinds of books, one of my favorite types, especially when I am on vacation or trying to relax, is well-written historical nonfiction. One of the most amazing historical books I've read in the last few years has to be Laura Hillenbrand's *Unbroken*.[6] The book tells the story of Louis Zamperini, a 1936 Olympian and World War II bombardier. His plane crashed in the Pacific Ocean, and he spent forty-seven days fighting off hunger and sharks. He then was interred in a Japanese prisoner-of-war camp for two years. If you have read the book, you know that the story is almost too unbelievable. It couldn't be a work of fiction, because it never would have made it past the editors. It actually happened.

I don't want to give away the rest of Hillenbrand's book, but sometimes when I am reading through the Old Testament, I am reminded of Zamperini's life. Just when you think there can't be another twist in the story or just when you think the characters are out of the woods, the bottom falls out again!

After the fall, it looked like the defeat of the Serpent might be around the corner with Abraham, but then his family ended up in slavery in Egypt. After the exodus from Egypt, God gave the people the law covenant, but they immediately broke it. When God put David on the throne, he and his sons sinned against God and failed to keep the covenant perfectly. And on and on it went. But in the midst of all of this, God was pointing forward to the solution to sin and death that he himself would provide. On the other side of that solution, God's people could finally look forward to returning to the blessings and joy of life in God's creation before sin crept into the picture.

To see this vision of what is in store for the people of God, we are actually going to backtrack a little bit and return to Isaiah's prophecies. In the last part of Isaiah, we get a glimpse of what God promised his people once the curse is finally removed:

> For behold, I create new heavens
>   and a new earth,
> and the former things shall not be remembered
>   or come into mind. (Isa. 65:17)

In our last stop, we saw that along with the new covenant, God's Spirit would breathe into his people—starting with the suffering servant—to give them new life. But this new life would not stop with the human race. God promised a new creation altogether, and Isaiah's prophecy paints a beautiful poetic picture of life in this new creation, the place where "the wolf and the lamb shall graze together" (v. 25).

But when he spoke of new heavens and a new earth, God probably did not mean that he is going to throw the old creation in the rubbish bin. Instead, he promised to remake it, renew it, and restore it. If you remember, back at the beginning of our journey, we saw God's strong commitment to his creation. In Genesis 1:31, he announced that it was very good, and even though the curse certainly changed it, the creation still reflects this proclamation in many ways. Because God has such a strong commitment to his creation, we see here that he is not willing to cast it aside, but will re-create it.

If we kept reading in Isaiah 65, we'd see that God's new creation will be the place where there is eternal joy (v. 18), no weeping or sadness (v. 19), true and lasting peace (v. 25), and joyful fellowship with God (v. 19). In other words, God's people will finally experience and enjoy the covenant blessing, dwelling with God forever, to its fullest. This chapter paints a picture of what it will look like when God has fully defeated the Serpent through the substitutionary sacrifice and Spirit-empowered life of the suffering servant. The effects of the curse will be finally and fully eradicated. Long before it ever happened, Isaiah's prophecies pointed forward to God's commitment to finish the work of redemption that he first promised in the garden.

Notice the second part of verse 17: "and the former things shall not be remembered or come into mind." Like the first part of the verse, I don't think we should assume that this part is implying that the new creation will sever all ties between the world we live in now and the world to come. It means that the pain, sin, and death that all came as a result of the curse will be wiped out.

All of the evil that the Serpent did and wanted to accomplish will be cast aside. The pain of disease and death brought on as a consequence of sin won't be in the picture any longer. The new covenant promises fulfilled through the life-giving Spirit will see to that.

In this new creation, God's people will once again live with him in the land that he is giving them. But this new creation will not be simply a restored garden of Eden. It will be much more. It will not be just a garden or even a nation stretching from Egypt to the Euphrates River. It will be the entire world! In this prophecy, it looks as if Isaiah was using Jerusalem and the new creation as synonyms. What will be true of the new creation will be true of the new Jerusalem, and vice versa. So here in Isaiah, the land that God promised to give his people is not just a nation, but actually the entire earth.

This shouldn't really surprise us, should it? God promised that all of the families of the earth would be blessed through Abraham. Later, we learned that the seed of Judah would be a king who would receive tribute from the nations. Then God made clear that Solomon's temple was to be a place of prayer for the nations to come. God never intended his people to come from one family, one ethnicity, or one nation. Just as the fall of Adam and Eve plunged the entire human race into sin, God's solution to the fall also has universal effects. While many tragically join the line of the Serpent and miss out on the blessing, the Old Testament is clear that no one nation— not even Israel—has an exclusive claim on God's promises. National borders will not contain his mercy. Even in the Old Testament, it is offered to all. In the new creation, his mercy will fill the earth as God lives among his people forever.

As we are nearing the end of the first part of our journey together, we need to step back and catch our breath. It has been a fast journey through the forest of the Old Testament, but we have seen eleven important trees that help us trace out the main story.

In the pages of the Old Testament, the first thirty-nine books of the Bible, we have the story of God's creation of all things, including the human race as the pinnacle of his creative work. The tragedy of the fall ripped Adam and Eve, along with all of their descendants, out of the presence of God and brought death to the world.

But God promised to crush the head of the Serpent and so redeem his people and his creation from the effects of the fall. In his covenants with Abraham, Israel, and David, we see that God was committed to restoring the blessing of his presence among all the peoples of the earth. Although sin and death kept rearing their ugly heads, the prophecies of Isaiah, Jeremiah, Ezekiel, and the rest of the prophets revealed that God would finally and fully defeat sin and death through a suffering servant who would represent his people. Then, and only then, would he renew and restore all creation, live among his people forever, and bring lasting joy and peace.

At this point in our journey, we are still looking forward. Those who heard these prophecies and took them to heart could only wait and see how and when they would be fulfilled. They knew God would do it, but they did not know who the servant would be and when he would defeat the Serpent and come out on the other side victorious.

The good news for us, though, is that we don't have to wait to hear the rest of the story. As we move into the New Testament, we will look at five key turning points that will help us see how the Old Testament promises were in fact fulfilled through the promised seed, the suffering servant, the resurrected Lord, Jesus Christ.

KEY BIBLICAL THEOLOGICAL THEMES

New creation

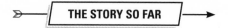

THE STORY SO FAR

God created a kingdom, and he is the King, but he made human beings to represent him in that kingdom. Adam and Eve rejected this call, which led to sin and death. But God promised to defeat the Serpent through the seed of the woman, who is also the seed of Abraham. Through Abraham's family, and specifically Judah's royal seed, David, the covenant blessings would come to the world. Because all people were guilty and deserved death, the sacrifices of the Mosaic law revealed more clearly their need for a substitute—the suffering servant. Through the servant and the work of the Spirit, God would establish a new covenant and give lasting life to his people in the new heavens and new earth.

PART 2

THE TIME
HAS COME

FULFILLMENT!

The time is fulfilled.

Mark 1:14–15

I have three young sons. As I write this, Luke, my oldest, is nine, Simon is five, and my youngest, Elliot, is three. Believe it or not, patience is not their strong suit. Most Sundays after church, they wait around while we help put away chairs or try to have a meaningful conversation with someone about what God is doing in his or her life. One or more of our boys is hungry. Or tired. Or thirsty. Or hot. Or cold. I can assure you that they didn't get their impatience from me—just don't ask my wife about that. The truth is, I am not the most patient of people. And for most people, waiting does not come naturally.

But waiting is exactly what God asked his people to do for about four centuries.

As the last Old Testament prophets—Haggai, Zechariah, and Malachi—completed their ministries, the people of God could look back through the ages and see how God had slowly revealed his plan for the promised seed to reverse the effects of the curse. Based on the unfolding covenant promises, they were looking for a new King David, God's Anointed One. In Hebrew, this Anointed One was called the *mashiach*, which is transliterated into English as "Messiah" and translated into Greek as *Christos*, or "Christ." This "messianic hope" was a right and proper expectation.

But in the shadow of these prophecies, there was also a strong expectation that when God defeated sin and death, he would also wipe out the geopolitical enemies of Israel. The people had expected freedom on the other side of their exile in Babylon, but after they returned home, a series of foreign armies ruled over the Israelites, or the Jews, as they came to be known. First, Alexander the Great conquered the nation, followed by a series of Greek and Egyptian rulers who kept the nation from regaining its independence. There was a short period of freedom under the Maccabees in the second century BC, but then the Romans seized control of the region. The great victory of God and his Messiah seemed a long way off.

But then another prophet came on the scene. He was not exactly the clean-cut type: "John was clothed with camel's hair and wore a leather belt around his waist and ate locusts and wild honey" (Mark 1:6). But his strange clothes and diet weren't the most amazing things about him. That was his message: he called the Jews to repent and told them that he was preparing the way for a greater prophet—a prophet who would baptize with the Holy Spirit (v. 8).

Now think back to what we saw in the Old Testament. The prophets foretold that when the Holy Spirit would come, he would bring with him the life and resurrection of the new covenant. Before that, the suffering servant would have to take on the sins of God's people as their representative. He was the one to whom all of the promises pointed. The promises to David, the Mosaic law, the promise to Judah, the covenant with

Abraham, and the promise that the seed of the woman would crush the Serpent's head all pointed to him! But we don't have to do all of that detective work. We can just keep reading Mark 1 to see this.

In verse 9, Mark tells us that Jesus of Nazareth came on the scene. If you've read the Gospels, you know that he was no ordinary man. He was born to Mary when she was still a virgin. From his earliest days, he knew that God was his Father in a very special way. In fact, we learn in John 1 that this man was none other than God incarnate. This should make sense. Who else could keep both sides of the covenants and pay the infinite debt that sin had brought? How else could God finally fulfill the promises except by becoming a man?

So this man, now grown, came to the Jordan River to be baptized. Then the Spirit of God, taking the form of a dove, descended on him, and the Father himself spoke from heaven to testify that Jesus was indeed his beloved Son. The three persons of the triune God, Father, Son and Holy Spirit, were all present, giving their approval to what Jesus was about to do.

Immediately after his baptism, Jesus—like the nation Israel after the exodus—went out into the wilderness. Since the Messiah was going to be the representative for the people, it shouldn't surprise us to see that he faced the temptations that they themselves faced. But unlike Israel of old, Jesus did not succumb to temptation in the wilderness. He came out on the other side victorious.

After Jesus's temptation, John "the Baptist" was arrested and executed. But anticipation still was building. John's followers were waiting to hear from Jesus. For those who had eyes to see, everything was pointing in one direction. But would John's prophecies and Jesus's actions just lead to more disappointment and waiting?

Finally, centuries after the promises to the last prophets,

a millennium and more after the promises to David, Judah, Abraham, and Adam, it happened. In our first stop in the New Testament, we see that Jesus came proclaiming the gospel, or good news, from God:

> Now after John was arrested, Jesus came into Galilee, proclaiming the gospel of God, and saying, "The time is fulfilled, and the kingdom of God is at hand; repent and believe in the gospel." (Mark 1:14–15)

His announcement of this news had three basic components. First, he said, "The time is fulfilled." Can you imagine the thrill of those who were waiting to see the fulfillment of all that God had promised? Imagine that you are one of them, and from as far back as you can remember, your grandfather has told you about the promises of God that he has been waiting for his whole life. He heard them from his grandfather, and his grandfather from his grandfather, and on and on for hundreds of years. But here was Jesus, standing in the wilderness in Galilee in the northern part of the Promised Land, announcing that the time had finally come!

If you are a J. R. R. Tolkien fan, you probably remember the anticipation leading up to the *Lord of the Rings* movies or, more recently, *The Hobbit*. After a year or more of waiting, you finally arrived early at the theater for the midnight screening, got your popcorn and maybe the 3-D glasses, and settled into your seat. As the lights went down and the movie started, you had a sense of excitement mingled with relief. It had finally come.

That feeling is only the slightest tip of the iceberg compared to the excitement and relief of those who finally saw the time of God's promises fulfilled. "The time is fulfilled" meant that the hopes of Adam and Eve, Abraham and the patriarchs, David and his son, all of the prophets, and all of those faithful Old Testament believers were finally being fulfilled! If you have been tracking the unfolding story of redemption, a similar thrill might well up in you as you read these words of Jesus.

Second, Jesus said, "the kingdom of God is at hand." The rule of God would finally be established, because the promised King who would perfectly keep God's law and perfectly reign over the people was finally present among them.

Jesus, as the anointed King, the Messiah, would succeed where Adam had failed. Even though Adam was the image of God, he did not rule God's kingdom as he should have. Neither did any of the kings in Israel or Judah. But finally here was One who would do what no other king could do. He would act as God's representative Ruler, the true King. But in order to establish his perfect reign, he would have to be the representative servant of God, which meant he would have to suffer on behalf of God's people. We will come back to that in our next text.

Finally, Jesus announced, "repent and believe in the gospel." In other words, the last part of his proclamation was a call to action. But it wasn't a call to political or military action, as many in his day expected from the Messiah. Instead, it was a call to do what God had commanded his people to do from the very beginning: they were to turn their backs on sin and believe that what he says is true.

This was a call for the people to trust that God would fulfill the covenant—that the way to finally be and do what he had called the human race to be and do would not come through their work, but instead through rest in him. Jesus, the representative of God's people, would do what they could not do for themselves—and he called them to believe that it was finally happening. The time that they had been waiting for had finally come!

You never thought so much excitement could be packed into two verses, did you? But as we will see in our next stop, this good news did not come without a cost.

KEY BIBLICAL THEOLOGICAL THEMES

Kingdom
Covenant
Redemption

THE STORY SO FAR

God created a kingdom, and he is the King, but he made human beings to represent him in that kingdom. Adam and Eve rejected this call, which led to sin and death. But God promised to defeat the Serpent through the seed of the woman, who is also the seed of Abraham. Through Abraham's family, and specifically Judah's royal seed, David, the covenant blessings would come to the world. Because all people were guilty and deserved death, the sacrifices of the Mosaic law revealed more clearly their need for a substitute—the suffering servant. Through the servant and the work of the Spirit, God would establish a new covenant and give lasting life to his people in the new heavens and new earth.

Jesus is the One through whom all of these promises find fulfillment.

THE CROSS

It is finished.

John 19:30

All the way back in Genesis 3, we saw that Adam and Eve failed to obey God and instead took the fruit from the tree of the knowledge of good and evil. Their refusal to obey at that tree destroyed the fellowship that they enjoyed with God, and the beauty and perfection of his creation was horribly scarred. But it was not hopelessly scarred. Before Adam and Eve could even begin to comprehend the new reality of life under the curse, God announced that there was a plan in place to make all things new again.

While we have seen this redemptive plan unfold at each stop of our tour through the Bible, we are finally arriving at its culmination. Again, we find ourselves looking up at a tree. Unlike that first tree in the garden, there was nothing attractive about this one. It had been stripped of its branches and shaped into a cross in order to be used for a crucifixion, the Romans' preferred method of execution for the worst of criminals. On that cross was the second person of the Trinity, the Son of God himself, who had become human in every sense of the word. The only person who had ever lived a truly innocent life was being executed in one of the worst ways possible. Yet it could not have been any other way. When he had made the payment for sin that God's people had needed all along, he said, "It is finished" and bowed his head, not in resignation, but in victory (John 19:30).

After Jesus announced the good news of God's fulfilled promises and the impending arrival of the kingdom, he spent about three years teaching and proclaiming this good news. As the long-awaited seed of the woman who would crush the head of the Serpent, he destroyed the works of the Devil and fought against the curse by casting out demons, healing the sick, and even raising the dead. As the seed of Abraham, he brought the blessing of God's presence back among his people. On some occasions, such as when he spoke to the Samaritan woman at the well (John 4), he began to bring that blessing of Abraham to all of the families of the earth. Unlike all of his ancestors before him, all the way back to Adam, Jesus perfectly kept the covenant with Israel, the law of God. He did all the things God had required of his people.

But there was a problem. After they had returned home from exile in Babylon, the Jews had rebuilt the temple and relaunched the sacrificial system. Once again, every year on the Passover, lambs were offered as substitutes for God's people. Again and again, the priests would slaughter the lambs as a reminder of God's justice and mercy. But the lambs still were not enough to pay the price for sin.

We saw in Isaiah 53 that the final substitute for the sins of God's people could not be a lamb. No, it had to be one of them. It had to be the Promised One, who would represent the people and stand in as their substitute. It shouldn't surprise us to hear Jesus say that his mission was not "to be served but to *serve*." His main task as a servant was "to give his life as a ransom for many" (Mark 10:45). When he said that, he was pointing back to Isaiah 53:11–12. He was the servant. Not only did he have to keep God's covenant perfectly so as to do what Adam, Abraham, Israel, and many others had failed to do; Jesus had to go one step further. He had to pay the penalty that all these, along with countless others, deserved for their sin.

And so to the cross he went. To most Jews in the first century, this was shocking and probably downright blasphemous. They had read the prophecies of God's Anointed One, the Messiah, but very few made the connection between the royal Son of David and the suffering servant. Because of this, most of them had no category for a suffering Messiah. The Messiah, they thought, would ride into Jerusalem as a conquering king and run the Romans out of town. Then he would conquer the Promised Land, reestablish the throne of David, and usher in a new golden age for Israel.

When rumors started circulating in the Judean countryside about a possible Messiah, the next logical step was seen as a revolt against Rome. After all, the people assumed, the only way Jesus could really prove that he was the Messiah was by defeating God's enemies. A few other guys who had claimed to be the Messiah had tried this tactic. These men tried to gather armies to defeat Rome, but, to a man, they were either run out of town or executed.

So as Jesus continued in his ministry, everyone was waiting for him to make his move on Rome. Finally, some of them thought it was coming. After a long journey from his home in Galilee, Jesus entered Jerusalem in the ancient equivalent of a ticker-tape parade. People were cutting palm branches down from the trees and waving them, literally throwing their clothes in the road to make a path for Jesus, and shouting:

"Hosanna! Blessed is he who comes in the name of the Lord!" (John 12:13). Every year, we remember this "Triumphal Entry" on Palm Sunday.

Jesus was indeed entering Jerusalem with victory on his mind, but it is unlikely that many of the folks who were celebrating that day understood what Jesus's victory would entail. Jesus never tried to conquer Rome, but as the week after his arrival went on, some of the Jewish leaders, along with Judas Iscariot, one of Jesus's followers, hatched a plot to kill him. Judas began looking for his chance.

Jesus knew he was heading toward the cross. Before he went, though, he wanted to celebrate the Passover meal with his closest followers. They followed the normal order of the meal, but when he broke the unleavened bread, Jesus said something strange: "This is my body" (Mark 14:22). Then, when they were drinking from the cup of wine together, he said, "This cup that is poured out for you is the new covenant in my blood" (Luke 22:20). He was saying that his broken body and spilled blood would fulfill the promise of the new covenant!

Soon after this, those same disciples saw the terrible price that had to be paid. Jesus was arrested, taken to the cross, and executed with two political terrorists—maybe guys who were looking for another messiah willing to take on Rome.

As he suffered on that cross, there is no doubt that Jesus was in physical anguish. But despite what the movies might lead you to believe, this was not his greatest pain. It came from being separated from God while bearing the weight of sin. As the suffering servant, he was the final substitute, the representative who took the weight of sin and the wrath of God on himself. He cried out in his spiritual and emotional anguish the words of Psalm 22:1: "My God, my God, why have you forsaken me?" (Mark 15:34). But that would not be his last word from the cross:

When Jesus had received the sour wine, he said, "It is finished," and he bowed his head and gave up his spirit. (John 19:30)

Finally, here was a sacrifice that would pay the price of sin once and for all. For centuries and centuries, the people of God had offered sacrifices that only pointed forward. Those sacrifices never finished the job. The next year, the next month, the next day there would be another sacrifice to offer. But no longer. As the end drew near, in spite of his anguish, in spite of his pain, Jesus could confidently say, "*It is finished.*"

In his suffering with those criminals, "they made his grave with the wicked," and in his burial in the tomb of the wealthy Joseph of Arimathea, he was "with a rich man in his death" (Isa. 53:9). In big and small details, Jesus perfectly fulfilled the prophecies of the suffering servant.

Finally, the strange vision of the divided animal that God had given to Abraham all those years before was fulfilled. Just as he had said he would, God had suffered the penalty due to all of us who break his laws and ignore his covenant. He himself had paid the price. One of Jesus's disciples with him that night would later write, "He himself bore our sins in his body on the tree, that we might die to sin and live to righteousness" (1 Pet. 2:24).

But that would not be the end of the story, because even as Jesus cried out in anguish as God forsook him, he knew the end of Psalm 22. Later in this psalm, which begins with a cry of despair, David wrote, "He has not despised or abhorred the affliction of the afflicted, and he has not hidden his face from him, but has heard, when he cried to him" (Ps. 22:24). Because it was finished, because the price for sin had been paid, the Serpent was defeated and the power of death was destroyed. Three days later, Jesus's followers saw this firsthand.

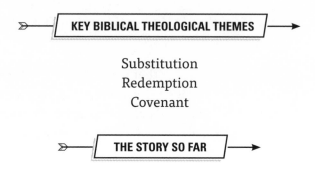

KEY BIBLICAL THEOLOGICAL THEMES

Substitution
Redemption
Covenant

THE STORY SO FAR

God created a kingdom, and he is the King, but he made human beings to represent him in that kingdom. Adam and Eve rejected this call, which led to sin and death. But God promised to defeat the Serpent through the seed of the woman, who is also the seed of Abraham. Through Abraham's family, and specifically Judah's royal seed, David, the covenant blessings would come to the world. Because all people were guilty and deserved death, the sacrifices of the Mosaic law revealed more clearly their need for a substitute—the suffering servant. Through the servant and the work of the Spirit, God would establish a new covenant and give lasting life to his people in the new heavens and new earth.

Jesus is the One through whom all of these promises find fulfillment, first in his sacrificial death for sin.

RESURRECTION

Declared to be the Son of God in power.

Romans 1:3–4

Hundreds of years before Jesus died on a cross, God asked the prophet Ezekiel, "Can these bones live?" The first answer to this question—a resounding yes—should have helped God's people to see that on the other side of the darkness of death, there is great hope. Yet, as two of Jesus's followers were walking from Jerusalem to Emmaus on the third day after his crucifixion, they did not seem to grasp that hope. They said, "We had hoped that he was the one to redeem Israel" (Luke 24:21). But their hope seemed to have died with him. Those men did not spend much time asking, "Can these bones live?" But on the third day that Jesus lay in the tomb, God gave us the decisive answer to that question.

The Gospels of Matthew, Mark, Luke, and John all end with the same event: the resurrection of Jesus and its immediate aftermath. Jesus was the first person to truly defeat death. Because of this, we have to conclude that in the resurrection of

Jesus, God started to fulfill his end-time promises to Ezekiel. In the resurrection, God gave new life to the One representative of his people, and in the wake of that, all those who are united to him share this life. To understand what happened in that garden tomb, however, we are not going to stop in the Gospels. Instead, we need to jump ahead to the letters of Paul.

If you stop and think about it, it is remarkable that Paul wrote about Jesus's resurrection. For the first year or two after Jesus's death and resurrection, the Pharisee Saul spent most of his waking hours working to wipe out the little group who would later be called Christians. But then Jesus met him on the road to Damascus, where Saul had planned to ambush a group of Christians. From then on, Saul, whose name was changed to Paul, became God's chosen instrument for taking the good news to the entire Mediterranean world.

Several decades after he met Jesus on the road to Damascus, Paul was preparing to take the gospel to Spain, the western edge of the Mediterranean world. But to get there, he needed to be sent out from Rome. So he wrote to the Christians in Rome to introduce himself. In the introduction to that letter, he gives a concise theological description of several paths that intersect at the resurrection. The Messiah, he says, is:

> [God's] Son, who was descended from David according to the flesh and was declared to be the Son of God in power according to the Spirit of holiness by his resurrection from the dead, Jesus Christ our Lord. (Rom. 1:3–4)

Paul first reminds us of one of the reasons why it was necessary for Jesus to rise from the dead. Jesus was "descended from David according to the flesh." He was the royal Son of David and the heir of all the promises that God gave to David. Remember that one of the promises to David was that God would "establish the throne of his kingdom forever" (2 Sam. 7:13).

Obviously the promise could not apply to Jesus if he were not alive to reign.

David's son Solomon and several other kings in Judah experienced a small taste of what it meant when God said, "I will be to him a father, and he shall be to me a son" (2 Sam. 7:14). But before Jesus, no king had fully experienced this. All of the kings before him had tasted God's discipline when they failed to obey him. Jesus never failed to obey, perfectly kept the covenant, and so proved that he was the Son of God in every sense of the phrase.

Even if you don't know us, you could look at my three sons and notice they have the same build, the same eyes, the same hair, and the same facial features as me. In other words, you could plainly see that they are my sons. If this is true of my sons, think of how much more we should be able to recognize the perfect Son. If we know the Father, we should know the Son, because the Son, in his life and conduct, resembled the Father.

But then, if we keep reading in Romans 1, Paul adds that Jesus "was declared to be the Son of God in power . . . by his resurrection." Now, you might be thinking to yourself, "Wait a second—wasn't Jesus God's Son from eternity?" And you are absolutely right—Jesus was, and is, the eternal Son of God, the second person of the Trinity. It is essential to get this right.

At the resurrection, we see the eternal Son of God publicly declared to be the messianic Son of God, just as his ancestor David was. For God to declare that David was his son meant that David and his descendants would be his closest allies and the ones through whom he would advance his saving plan. So just as you might identify my sons because they look like and act like me, you identify God's Son because he does what God does. He rescues God's people and saves them from sin and death.

The resurrection, therefore, was proof that Jesus was the true Son of David, the true seed of the woman. At the resurrection, millennia of promises were confirmed. The King had come, had paid the price to redeem his people, and had come out on the other side of death victorious. Because of this, it could finally be said of this Son of David that his throne would be established forever!

In the last part of Paul's description, we see the role that the Holy Spirit plays in the resurrection—just as God had revealed to Ezekiel: "according to the Spirit of holiness by his resurrection from the dead." The resurrection of Jesus was the first fulfillment of God's promise to breathe new life into his people and to pour out his Spirit on his people. In Jesus's resurrection, the Spirit gave new life to the One representative and focal point of these promises.

Jesus's death and resurrection were together the turning point in history. These connected events had cosmic implications that trickle down into every nook and cranny of our everyday existence. Although we see the culmination of God's saving promises in Jesus, the resurrected, Spirit-anointed Son of David, we also know that those promises did not stop with Jesus. His resurrection was just the beginning.

Most people don't stop and consider this, but it was shocking for Jesus's followers to see his resurrection without also seeing the transformation of creation and the renewal of all things that we saw prophesied in Isaiah 65. They expected it all to happen at once, but we can now see that these promises are being fulfilled in stages over time. It is often said that these promises are a bit like looking at a mountain range from a distance. As you get closer to the mountains, you discover that what looks like a single mountain from several miles away is actually a series of smaller peaks that lead to the highest point. In the same way, what looked like a single end-time event from the perspective of the readers of the Old Testament was actually a series of mountain peaks. And the first of those peaks, the one that actually makes the rest of them possible, is the death and resurrection of Jesus.

This means that Jesus's death and resurrection launched the end-of-time fulfillment of God's saving promises. You might sometimes hear theologians talking about "inaugurated eschatology." They are describing exactly what we have been talking about here. They simply mean that Jesus has already started to fulfill everything the Old Testament pointed us toward. His death and resurrection constituted the decisive blow to sin and death; by them, he crushed the Serpent's head.

And not only this, but the good news of his victory over sin and death is going to the nations, so the blessing of Abraham is reaching all the families of the earth. In his perfect keeping of the covenant in his life and sacrificial death, he fulfilled everything that the law was intended to do. He is now reigning as the Davidic King, the descendent of Judah who is honored among the nations. This is why Paul could say in another letter, "If anyone is in Christ, the new creation has come!" (2 Cor. 5:17 NIV). Jesus has done everything necessary for the new creation to come.

While Jesus's death and resurrection won the long-awaited victory over the curse, we are constantly reminded that the effects of the fall are still very much among us. Even as I type these words, I hear sirens in the distance. Somewhere out my window, someone is sick, hurt, or dying.

Not long ago, I saw a YouTube video of a decapitated snake's head, and yes, it was about as gross as it sounds. When the guy holding the camera got too close, the head actually lunged toward him and tried to bite him! Apparently some snakes have a sort of heat sensor in their jaws, and this defensive mechanism keeps working for several hours after they die. If you are not careful, this can have deadly results. Just recently, a chef in China was making soup with a spitting cobra (I'd recommend not trying that at home). He cut off the snake's head and continued preparing the meal. But twenty minutes later, when he went to throw it in the trash, the severed head bit him, and he died. Even a dead snake's head can still do some damage! So Jesus's victory over sin and his new creation *already* have been settled, but we do *not yet* see their full results.

After he rose from the grave, Jesus did not march back into Jerusalem and take vengeance on the Roman and Jewish leaders. He quietly appeared to his followers and taught them the significance of his resurrection—that God is giving life to dead, dry bones. He joined those two followers on the road to Emmaus and helped them see the ways in which all of the promises of God and the entire story of Scripture point to him. He helped them see that it was necessary for the Messiah to die and rise again for his people. He helped them to see that the new creation had indeed come. And then, forty days after he rose from the dead, Jesus ascended to heaven.

But soon after that, we discover in Acts, he sent the Holy Spirit to keep bringing life from the dead. And he has called his people to extend this saving message to the nations and gather people from all over the earth to experience the blessing of Abraham. So at our next tree, we will move forward a couple of chapters in Romans and unpack this saving message and some of its implications before we finally reach the glorious end of our journey.

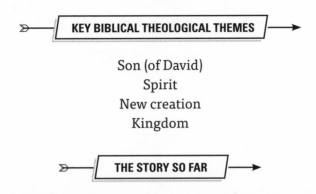

KEY BIBLICAL THEOLOGICAL THEMES

Son (of David)
Spirit
New creation
Kingdom

THE STORY SO FAR

God created a kingdom, and he is the King, but he made human beings to represent him in that kingdom. Adam and Eve rejected this call, which led to sin and death. But God promised to defeat the Serpent through the seed of the woman, who is also the seed of Abraham. Through Abraham's family, and specifically Judah's royal seed, David, the covenant blessings would come to the world. Because all people were guilty and deserved death, the sacrifices of the Mosaic law revealed more clearly their need for a substitute—the suffering servant. Through the servant and the work of the Spirit, God would establish a new covenant and give lasting life to his people in the new heavens and new earth.

Jesus is the One through whom all of these promises find fulfillment, first in his sacrificial death for sin and then in his victorious resurrection and reign as King.

JUSTIFICATION

So that he might be just and the justifier
of the one who has faith in Jesus.

Romans 3:21–26

With apologies to my dendrologist friends reading this book, most trees are pretty boring (and if you are wondering, yes, I had to do some research to learn that a person who studies trees is a dendrologist). Most trees are basically the same: each has a trunk, a few branches, leaves, maybe some fruit or nuts, and that's about it. So while we've used the "forest and trees" analogy throughout this book, I haven't tried to overthink it by comparing Genesis 3:15 to an apple tree and Mark 1:15 to a palm tree. A tree is a tree.

But there is one kind of tree that I actually do find pretty interesting. The banyan tree is, for lack of a better word, one of the most *complicated* trees I've ever seen. A banyan tree often starts off when a banyan seed falls onto a branch of another type of tree, germinates, and starts to grow out in all directions. Once the root reaches the ground, it plants itself in the soil with a whole new root system as it intersects with other banyan roots. Over time, the roots wind around each other and grow larger and larger as they grow together. The end result is a complex series of interconnected roots both in and out of the ground. In fact, if you ever make it to Lahaina, Maui, check out a single banyan tree there that has grown to cover more than half an acre of land. It's pretty amazing.

The next tree in our look at the forest of the Bible's storyline is kind of like a banyan tree. Paul's short summary of the gospel message in Romans 3 has a series of interconnected roots that have grown together to form a single tree:

> But now the righteousness of God has been manifested apart from the law, although the Law and the Prophets bear witness to it—the righteousness of God through faith in Jesus Christ for all who believe. For there is no distinction: for all have sinned and fall short of the glory of God, and are justified by his grace as a gift, through the redemption that is in Christ Jesus, whom God put forward as a propitiation by his blood, to be received by faith. This was to show God's righteousness, because in his divine forbearance he had passed over former sins. It was to show his righteousness at the present time, so that he might be just and the justifier of the one who has faith in Jesus. (Rom. 3:21–26)

In this chapter, we need to unpack the key statements found in this glorious summary. Get your thinking caps out.

"But now the righteousness of God has been manifested apart from the law, although the Law and the Prophets bear witness to it . . ."

After explaining the need for Christ in the first part of this epistle, Paul begins his summary of the good news in Romans by affirming that God's righteousness—particularly as it is on display in the life, death, and resurrection of Jesus—is revealed apart from the law and its stipulations. However, the entire Old Testament ("the Law and the Prophets" was a common way to refer to the Old Testament for Paul) testifies about God's righteousness.

". . . the righteousness of God through faith in Jesus Christ for all who believe. For there is no distinction: for all have sinned and fall short of the glory of God, and are justified by his grace as a gift . . ."

Just in case anyone misunderstands, Paul emphasizes that the righteousness of God he has in mind here is that which comes to God's people through faith in Jesus Christ. As you hope in Jesus Christ as the only substitute for your sin and cast yourself on him, God righteously declares you "not guilty" and welcomes you into his kingdom. Don't forget the history of Israel and begin to think that you can somehow fix your sin problem or anyone else's. You need the substitute to do it for you!

The need for a substitute is universal. We saw this in Exodus, when both Israelites and Egyptians were under God's judgment. *All* have sinned—Jew and Gentile, rich and poor, educated and uneducated, men, women, and children. No one escapes the curse, and everyone is robbing God of the glory he deserves as our Creator and King.

This means that people are justified—declared to be righteous before God—only by his grace. Abraham did not earn the right to be the father of the Promised One. The Israelites did not escape from Egypt because they were so much better than the Egyptians. David did not merit God's favor when God promised him an eternal throne. In the same way, neither you, I, nor anyone you know deserves God's favor. His grace is just that—grace, unearned favor. God's kindness in the story of the Bible is astonishing!

". . . through the redemption that is in Christ Jesus, whom

God put forward as a propitiation by his blood, to be received by faith."

This justification, Paul explains, is based on the work of the Messiah, Jesus. He redeems us by his blood. The Passover lambs purchased Israel's salvation so they would not have to face the judgment that they deserved, but those sacrifices were not finally effective. As we saw in chapter 13, Jesus came to finish those sacrifices and pay the debt we all owed.

Paul calls this payment "propitiation." This theological word simply refers to something—or someone—that appeases God's righteous wrath. While many people don't like to talk about the wrath of God, we cannot really get around it without distorting the message of the Bible. Sin is not just a minor inconvenience. When we sin, we are shaking our fists at the God who made us, telling him that we doubt that he is good and don't believe that he can be trusted. Part of God's righteousness is his wrath toward this insolence. When we put our sin in proper perspective, God would be unrighteous *not* to judge it.

We recognize the need for justice in the worst crimes. In our world, the Nazis are almost a cliché, but the truth is, they murdered more than six million people. From November 1945 to October 1946, the Allied forces held a series of military tribunals to prosecute the Nazi war criminals for their part in this terrible Holocaust. During the trials, twelve prominent Nazi leaders were sentenced to death. But imagine if the Allies had simply decided to pardon the masterminds behind the deaths of so many, give them a new start, and allow them to walk free with no consequences. This would have been a travesty! Likewise, when we truly understand the nature of our sin against God, we see that it cannot be swept under the carpet.

God's righteous wrath is not the equivalent of one of us throwing a little tantrum because we don't get our way. Let's not make the mistake of thinking that God is like us. Instead, think about the way you feel when you see an undeniable injustice or hear of the exploitation of children. Something wells up in you that says, "This is not the way things ought to be!" When we defy the God who made us to love him, worship him, and live with him, his only just and proper response is wrath against our treason and our injustice. So apart from the sacrifice of the perfect Lamb, the suffering servant, God would be unjust to welcome us.

"This was to show God's righteousness, because in his divine forbearance he had passed over former sins. It was to show his righteousness at the present time, so that he might be just and the justifier of the one who has faith in Jesus."

So, Paul concludes, Jesus's death was absolutely necessary in order for God to accept us and remain truly righteous.

God could have immediately and decisively judged all of the sins committed from the garden of Eden to the cross of Christ. The reality is, God would be perfectly righteous to strike you down and send you to hell the moment you envy your neighbor, lust after your coworker, or doubt his kindness to you. But in his "divine forbearance," he has not struck you down. This is why Paul could say in the previous chapter of Romans that "God's kindness is meant to lead you to repentance" (Rom. 2:4). For year after year, with sacrifice after sacrifice, God was patiently passing over sin.

For God to be just, however, someone had to pay for that sin. And now, in this era after the cross, we see who that someone is. Jesus paid the price that we deserved for our sin. Because Jesus did this, God can actually forgive us without any stain on his character or sense of injustice.

In truth, we all deserve death without mercy. But God, who is rich in mercy, has unfolded this amazing plan of redemption. Through Jesus, he has decisively defeated sin and death and has brought us back to what we were created for: living with God forever in the world he created for his glory. This is where the story has been heading all along: back to the place we were created to live, back to paradise, back to the presence of God, forever.

KEY BIBLICAL THEOLOGICAL THEMES

Redemption
Sin
Judgment
Substitution

THE STORY SO FAR

God created a kingdom, and he is the King, but he made human beings to represent him in that kingdom. Adam and Eve rejected this call, which led to sin and death. But God promised to defeat the Serpent through the seed of the woman, who is also the seed of Abraham. Through Abraham's family, and specifically Judah's royal seed, David, the covenant blessings would come to the world. Because all people were guilty and deserved death, the sacrifices of the Mosaic law revealed more clearly their need for a substitute—the suffering servant. Through the servant and the work of the Spirit, God would establish a new covenant and give lasting life to his people in the new heavens and new earth.

Jesus is the One through whom all of these promises find fulfillment, first in his sacrificial death as a necessary and just payment for sin and then in his victorious resurrection and reign as King.

GLORY

The dwelling place of God is with man.

Revelation 21:1–4

Not long after we started thinking about God and his very good creation, it seemed as if the problem of sin and death took us on an immediate detour. But as we look back at the amazing story of salvation that we have traced together, I hope you see that this was no detour. From the very beginning, God intended for us to behold his glory in his astonishing plan to save undeserving sinners; and from the very beginning, God intended to send his own Son to die for the ungodly. The promises in the Old Testament, the sacrifices of the law, everything that prophets such as Isaiah and Ezekiel spoke about, along with everything else in the Old Testament found its fulfillment in Jesus. He came to do for us what we could never do for ourselves, and as a result, he defeated the problem of sin and death and crushed the Serpent's head.

But this story did not end two thousand years ago. You and I have been called to be a part of it! Forty days after his resurrection, Jesus ascended into heaven. Then the good news about Jesus, the seed of the woman, the reigning Son of David, burst out of Jerusalem and started spreading around the world. And it's been on the move ever since. From the resurrection until the return of Christ, this amazing story continues whenever the gospel goes to a new place. We are called to bring the good news of God's saving plan to those around us who are hurting, still lost in sin and death.

However, this won't go on forever and ever. The New Testament is full of promises that, as the angels told the disciples watching Jesus ascend to heaven, he will "come in the same way as you saw him go into heaven" (Acts 1:11). Jesus is coming back!

Lots of Christians disagree about the details of Christ's return, but they all agree that when he comes, his people will live with him forever. They all agree that when he comes, sin and death will be finally and fully defeated, and the Devil and everyone who follows him will face the just consequences for their rebellion and treason against God. So will those who continue to shake their fists at God, not believing him, not trusting that he really is enough. But those who cast themselves on Jesus will live with him forever in the new creation that we saw back in Isaiah.

While Isaiah 65 gave us our first glimpse at those days, we find the culmination of that vision in the last book of the Bible, Revelation. As we finish our journey, let's take a few moments to rejoice in what awaits us. God's people will finally live with God, uncorrupted by sin and death, unharried by worry and pain, unconcerned about whether and how we can earn God's favor. God's people will live with him under the perfect rule of Jesus:

> Then I saw a new heaven and a new earth, for the first heaven and the first earth had passed away, and the sea

was no more. And I saw the holy city, new Jerusalem, coming down out of heaven from God, prepared as a bride adorned for her husband. And I heard a loud voice from the throne saying, "Behold, the dwelling place of God is with man. He will dwell with them, and they will be his people, and God himself will be with them as their God. He will wipe away every tear from their eyes, and death shall be no more, neither shall there be mourning, nor crying, nor pain anymore, for the former things have passed away." (Rev. 21:1–4)

In this vision, John saw a new heaven and a new earth—a new creation. Let's just get this out of the way now: heaven will not be an eternity of boredom, sitting on clouds and mindlessly strumming harps. The more I read the Bible, the more "earthy" I'm convinced that heaven will be. It will be a vibrant, joy-filled place where every one of our senses will be fully engaged. Next time you are gazing at a beautiful sunset or a snowcapped mountain, just remember that there is a new creation still to come. Until we are there, we won't really understand what it means to live in and truly enjoy God's creation.

The new creation will also be a place where danger, fear, and anxiety will be gone forever—this is what John means by "the sea was no more." Now, I used to live in Hawai'i, so when most of my friends there see that there will be no sea, they get a little worried! How can we really enjoy creation without surfing, diving, or swimming?

If you are thinking this, let me try to set your mind at ease. In the ancient world, water sports had not exactly taken off. Even among those few who actually had time for recreational sports, very few were going into the water. Instead, for most people, the sea was a picture of danger and the unknown. So instead of thinking about all of the fun they'd miss out on with no ocean to play in, John's readers would have thought of all the potential danger they'd be spared with no sea to worry about. We get a sense of this in the last part of our passage: "He will wipe away every tear from their eyes, and death shall be no more, neither shall there be mourning, nor crying, nor pain anymore, for the former things have passed away."

"The former things," all the fallout from sin and death, will pass away. The curse will be irreversibly crushed, and we will experience what Adam and Eve were only beginning to taste in the garden.

Also, notice that we will live in "the holy city, new Jerusalem." Remember how Isaiah saw the new creation and the new Jerusalem as two ways of talking about the same thing? John is following his lead here and seeing the two as identical. God seems to take the kernel of the promise and multiply it exponentially.

If we stop and think about it, this is pretty amazing and actually summarizes the way we've seen God work throughout the Bible. The promises to Abraham included the promise to bless all the families of the earth. While we never lost sight of that worldwide promise, the line of promise narrowed to one nation, one family, and eventually one person. But we finally see the full scope of God's worldwide promise here in Revelation. So it makes sense that Jerusalem, the city where God's people and, more importantly, his presence dwelt, will one day fill the whole earth, because we see that the dwelling place of God will permanently be with man (v. 3). God's promises were never intended for one nation or ethnic group. As John saw earlier in Revelation, the Lamb of God "ransomed people for God from every tribe and language and people and nation" (Rev. 5:9).

Because God will live there and every threat that sin has raised will be expelled, this new creation will be far beyond anything we can imagine. It certainly won't be boring, but it will be beautiful, like "a bride adorned for her husband." If you are a husband, you know that in those moments when you watched your bride walk down the aisle, you could not think of anything more beautiful.

Our experience in the new creation will be similarly joyful, even though we will be the bride, not the Bridegroom. Because of the work of Jesus, our Messiah and King, we finally will live as God intended, under his perfect rule, in the place he prepared for us, living with him forever. Here, finally, the covenants with Abraham, Judah, Israel, and David will see their fulfillment as the royal offspring reigns forever over God's redeemed people.

Throughout this book, we have been using the metaphor of the forest and the trees, and we can actually summarize the story of the Bible by looking at three real trees. We saw in Genesis 3 that Adam and Eve sinned when they took the fruit from the tree of the knowledge of good and evil. This plunged the world into sin and death, but God immediately began working to send the seed of the woman to reverse the curse. As we learned in John 19, Jesus did this and paid the decisive price for sin when he gave his body on the tree of Calvary. Finally, here in Revelation, we find a third tree.

If we keep reading in Revelation, we find the tree of life springing up in the middle of this city. A river that flows from the very throne of God feeds this tree, and the tree gives life to the nations (Rev. 22:1–2). As it was at the very beginning, God's people will always be dependent on him for life. But we have seen that he can always be trusted to give what we need. And for all of eternity, we will have the joy of trusting him and receiving from him. This is what we were made for—to live in and enjoy the life-giving presence of God.

So this story is not just a story we sit back and read to our kids. It is a story that you and I are called to join. Jesus said,

"Behold, I am making all thing new" (Rev. 21:5). Right now, he is making new creatures as more and more people around the world put their hope in him as their only Savior. And he calls us to proclaim that good news to this world that is still suffering in sin and death. We have the joy of seeing God at work to reverse the curse and defeat the Serpent. We get to announce the good news of Jesus's victory and invite our neighbors and friends to turn from their sin and trust in him alone as their substitute and Savior. So put down this book and get to work—he has called you to join this mission!

KEY BIBLICAL THEOLOGICAL THEMES

New creation
Kingdom
Covenant
Seed

THE STORY SO FAR

God created a kingdom, and he is the King, but he made human beings to represent him in that kingdom. Adam and Eve rejected this call, which led to sin and death. But God promised to defeat the Serpent through the seed of the woman, who is also the seed of Abraham. Through Abraham's family, and specifically Judah's royal seed, David, the covenant blessings would come to the world. Because all people were guilty and deserved death, the sacrifices of the Mosaic law revealed more clearly their need for a substitute—the suffering servant. Through the servant and the work of the Spirit, God would establish a new covenant and give lasting life to his people in the new heavens and new earth.

Jesus is the One through whom all of these promises find fulfillment, first in his sacrificial death as a necessary and just payment for sin and then in his victorious resurrection and reign as King. This great story will find its culmination when the redeemed from every tribe, tongue, and nation gather in the new creation to live with God forever.

Where to Go Next

Whether you've been reading the Bible your entire life or just picked it up for the first time while reading this book, I hope that you have gotten a better handle on the overall story and the unity of God's Word. I also hope that this book has not exhausted your desire to learn biblical theology. Hopefully, at this point, you are asking, what should I read next?

Start by reading your Bible. Try to make it through the entire Bible every year. As you do so with this story in mind, you will start to make connections with what you've read here (or corrections to it!). You will find that I have left out many parts of the story.

After the Bible, let me recommend just three books. These books will point you to other books, and they will point you to others, and so on:

- Graeme Goldsworthy, *According to Plan: The Unfolding Revelation of God in the Bible* (IVP Academic, 2002), 251 pages. Goldsworthy will give you a fuller picture of the story of the Bible and will help fill in the gaps that our short overview of the Bible had to pass over.
- Michael Lawrence, *Biblical Theology in the Life of the Church: A Guide for Ministry* (Crossway, 2010), 240 pages. Lawrence will help you get a better handle on how the study of biblical theology fits with other theological study and, most importantly, help you see its vital role in your life and ministry in your own church.

- Thomas R. Schreiner, *The King in His Beauty: A Biblical Theology of the Old and New Testaments* (Baker Academic, 2013), 736 pages. You can see by the page count that this book is not for the faint of heart—but it is worth the work. Schreiner's biblical theology will take you on a book-by-book tour of the Bible, unpacking the unfolding story and helping you to see comprehensively both the parts and the whole. Since this book walks sequentially through the Bible, try reading it alongside your Bible one year.

Notes

1. John Milton, *Paradise Lost*, 10.585–90.
2. William Cowper, "God Moves in a Mysterious Way," 1774.
3. It is not entirely clear what the name *Sarai* means and whether it has a substantially different meaning from *Sarah*. At the least, we can say this new name added emphasis to Sarah's role as mother of the nation.
4. C. S. Lewis, *Prince Caspian* (New York: HarperTrophy, 2000), 69.
5. If you don't believe me, read Ezekiel 20:4–32. Even when they were slaves in Egypt, God said, the Israelites would not forsake the gods of the Egyptians.
6. Laura Hillenbrand, *Unbroken: A World War II Story of Survival, Resilience, and Redemption* (New York: Random House, 2010).

General Index

Scripture Index

Download a free study guide for

THE WHOLE STORY OF THE BIBLE IN
16 VERSES

crossway.org/16versesSG

The Importance of Church Partnerships for the Sake of the Gospel

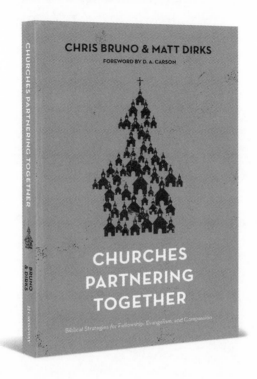

"God can and does work miracles through local churches linked together by the gospel for the sake of loving their communities by introducing them to Jesus. I love the vision Chris and Matt live out and lay out in this book. May their tribe increase!"

COLLIN HANSEN, Editorial Director, The Gospel Coalition; coauthor, *A God-Sized Vision: Revival Stories That Stretch and Stir*

"I welcome this new book. The rising generation of young evangelicals needs to embrace once again a fully biblical understanding of cooperation so churches united in faith can cooperate together to share the gospel with the world."

R. ALBERT MOHLER JR., President and Joseph Emerson Brown Professor of Christian Theology, The Southern Baptist Theological Seminary

For more information, visit crossway.org.